COLUMBIA UNIVERSITY GERMANIC STUDIES

THE SOLILOQUY IN GERMAN DRAMA

THE SOLILOQUY
IN GERMAN DRAMA

BY

ERWIN W. ROESSLER

AMS PRESS, INC.
NEW YORK
1966

Approved for publication, on behalf of the Department of Germanic Languages and Literatures of Columbia University.

CALVIN THOMAS.

NEW YORK, December, 1914

TO

MY PARENTS

WHOSE SELF-DENIAL MADE POSSIBLE MY EDUCATION

CONTENTS

INTRODUCTION

In the family of dramatic conventions no member has played so important a role, and on the other hand none has had so ignominious an ending, after a most glorious career, as the soliloquy. In its present crushed and lowly estate, it forcibly reminds one of the last years of the great exile at St. Helena. After centuries of the greatest popularity with both playwright and audience, the soliloquy has at last met with the fate of most popular idols and been ruthlessly ousted from its comfortable throne.

This revulsion of feeling occurred in the final decades of the nineteenth century, when "the leading playwrights of every modern language began to display a distaste for the monolog, with Ibsen setting the example of renunciation."[1] There seems to be a consensus of opinion regarding Ibsen's stimulating influence on the technic of modern drama,[2] an influence which manifested itself particularly in the disappearance of the soliloquy from the drama. Mr. Hamilton says: "The present prevalence of objection to soliloquy and aside is due largely to the strong influence of Ibsen's rigid dramaturgic structure."[3] Mr. Henderson, commenting upon Ibsen's remark that his "League of Youth" is written "without a single monolog, in fact, without a single aside," declares: "In this respect, I believe Ibsen sounded the deathknell of the monolog, the soliloquy, the aside, and by his practice soon rendered ridiculous those dramatists who persisted in employing these devices."[4]

[1] A Study of the Drama, by Brander Matthews, New York, 1910, p. 142.

[2] The Development of the Drama, by Brander Matthews, New York, 1906, pp. 37, 321, 326, 349. Der Monolog und Ibsen, by R. Franz, Marburg, 1907, p. 95. Die deutsche Literatur des 19. Jahrhunderts, R. M. Meyer, Berlin, 1906, pp. 709, 787, etc.

[3] Theory of the Theatre, by Clayton Hamilton, New York, 1910, p. 88.

[4] The Evolution of Dramatic Technic, by Archibald Henderson, North American Review, March, 1909, p. 439. For this and a few other citations I am indebted to Mr. Arnold's monograph on The Soliloquies of Shakespeare. New York, 1911.

1

R. V. Gottschall repeatedly rails at Ibsen for having given the soliloquy its deathblow.[1]

Professor Brander Matthews admits that Ibsen "has been masterly in his adjustment of his methods to the conditions of the picture-frame stage,"[2] but shifts the real responsibility for the disappearance of the soliloquy a little further back upon Edison's shoulders, as the introduction of electric lighting together with the picture-frame stage created a setting so realistic that the stepping out of the picture to talk intimately with the audience was felt to be entirely out of place. The fact remains, however, that Ibsen was the first to realize this inappropriateness and, having realized it, to perfect a new techinc that discarded soliloquies and asides. Accordingly he is entitled to the greatest credit.

Before discussing the various types of soliloquy and quoting the opinions held by critics and poets regarding the value and justification of the same, a definition of the soliloquy might not be amiss.

St. Augustine coined the Latin *soliloquium* from *solus* and *loqui,* a "talking alone," from which the English form is derived.[3] The Standard Dictionary defines soliloquy as a talking to one's self regardless of the presence or absence of others, a discourse uttered for one's own benefit. The French form *soliloque* is defined as the discourse of a person who talks to himself.[4] For some mysterious reason the German language has refused the rights of naturalization to the Latin applicant, and there seems to be but one instance[5] of its use and that in the Latin form. In the above definitions it is noteworthy that there is not the slightest suggestion of the stage or the drama.

Turning to the word *monolog,* from the Greek μόνος and λόγος, a "talking alone," what do we find? Oxford dictionary: " a scene in which a person of the drama speaks by himself; contrasted with chorus and dialogue." Standard: a dramatic solil-

[1] Zur Kritik des modernen Dramas, by R. v. Gottschall, Berlin, 1900, pp. 11, 119, 213.

[2] Matthews, A Study of the Drama, p. 64.

[3] W. W. Skeat, Etymological Dictionary.

[4] Nouveau Larousse, vol. 7.

[5] Bodmer in a letter to C. H. Miller, March 5, 1782.

oquy. Both add a modern use, viz., a dramatic composition for a single performer, a kind of dramatic entertainment performed throughout by one person, as, e. g., a monolog in vaudeville. The Encyclopedia Britannica, Meyer's and Brockhaus' Konversations-Lexika and La grande Encyclopédie all agree that a monolog is a passage in a dramatic piece in which a personage holds the scene to himself and speaks to himself. It would seem, then, that monolog and soliloquy, although etymologically equivalent, are not synonymous, inasmuch as the former refers to a portion of a drama, whereas the latter does not necessarily suggest the footlights. The difficulty can be peacefully settled, however, and both of the contestants put upon an equal footing by prefixing "dramatic" to soliloquy. Why English and American critics, with few exceptions,[1] have preferred the term soliloquy, in spite of the fact that all German[2] and French critics and dramatists have used *Monolog* and *monologue* respectively, is a question that I am unable to answer.

I should accordingly re-phrase Dr. Arnold's definition, "It is evident that all soliloquies are monologs, but that monologs are not necessarily soliloquies,"[3] as follows: Not all soliloquies are monologs, but monologs are necessarily dramatic soliloquies.

A dramatic soliloquy then is a passage in a drama in which a character is alone upon the stage and speaks to himself, believing himself to be alone. Even when the character is not alone on the stage his speech may be a soliloquy if it shows that the character is entirely oblivious to his surroundings.

How does the aside differ from the soliloquy? Mr. Paull,[4] Mr. Henderson[5] and Dr. Hennequin[6] maintain that it is nothing more than a short monolog. Inasmuch as the aside is a

---

[1] Dryden, Essay on Dramatic Poesy, 1668. Hédelin, The Whole Art of the Stage Made English, 1684. A. Hennequin, The Art of Playwriting, 1890.

[2] The word Selbstgespräch is occasionally used, but it may refer to a soliloquy off the stage as well as to a monolog.

[3] The Soliloquies of Shakespeare, p. 2.

[4] Dramatic Convention with Special Reference to the Soliloquy, Fortnightly Review, May, 1899, p. 863 ff.

[5] The Evolution of Dramatic Technic, North American Review, March, 1909, p. 432 ff.

[6] Art of Playwriting, p. 152 ff.

remark uttered by an actor on the stage so as not to be heard by other characters on the stage, it violates two of the principles of the monolog. The speaker of the aside is not alone on the stage, nor does he believe himself alone; he is not speaking to himself, but nearly always to the audience. The distinctive characteristic of the aside is that it occurs in the midst of dialog, although it is also regularly used in connection with the overheard soliloquy.

The overheard soliloquy, frequently employed in Roman comedy, crops out in large numbers in Gryphius's comedies and continues to be in vogue till Lessing's time—a good example occurs in "Der junge Gelehrte." Kleist makes use of this device on one occasion, but as a rule it has been tabooed by serious drama. It is, indeed, an "arrant absurdity, a contradiction in terms."[1] Inasmuch as the convention of the dramatic soliloquy is that the audience is permitted to overhear the thoughts of a character when he is alone on the stage, that the thoughts are made audible only for the audience, the absurdity of one actor actually overhearing another's thoughts becomes evident.

The definition of monolog and soliloquy, the former referring to the stage, the latter to real life, naturally suggests the question: To what extent is it natural to soliloquize off the stage? "No person in the full possession of his senses will utter more than short exclamations when he is alone. He may cry, sing, whistle, even laugh, mumble a few words, but never express what he feels, least of all what he intends to do."[2] Dr. Arnold says that it is undeniable that people do talk to themselves, but that it is preposterous "that young, healthy persons audibly set forth their secret ideas at great length."[3] I hardly believe that only the aged and infirm indulge in this peculiarity. Say what one will, the fact remains that a person who soliloquizes is considered peculiar, if not slightly demented. As Jean Paul puts it: "A person who in his waking moments talks to himself fills us with a shudder; and if I hear myself talking

---

[1] Brander Matthews, Putnam's Monthly, Nov., 1906, p. 183.
[2] R. Franz, Der Monolog und Ibsen, Marburg, 1907, p. 42.
[3] The Soliloquies of Shakespeare, p. 20.

when alone I have the same feeling."[1] Gottfried Keller in his autobiographical novel confesses: "I felt ashamed of myself; I could not hear myself talk alone and I was no longer able to pray aloud even in the deepest solitude and secrecy."[2] Heyse[3] refers to soliloquizing as a weakness; Dostojewsky[4] refers to a soliloquizer as a hypochondriac. Paull tersely says: "A man does not speak to himself, unless indeed he is beside himself."[5]

But—*altera pars audiatur!* For the soliloquy has champions as well as sarcastic defamers. Diderot, in his essay on dramatic poetry, writes: "You know that I have long been in the habit of soliloquizing. When I return home sad and chagrined I retire to my study and there I question myself and ask: what ails you?"[6] Marmontel in his "Poétique" defends the soliloquy in ardent fashion: "It is entirely natural to speak to one's self. There is not a person who does not find himself talking to himself at times about matters that affect or seriously interest him."[7] Nicolai maintains that it is not contrary to nature for a person who is aroused or excited to talk to himself.[8] Henderson grants that "people sometimes—and not infrequently—do give audible expression to their thoughts and feelings."[9] According to H. Gartelmann it is "a well known phenomenon that people not infrequently begin to think aloud, to soliloquize, when greatly moved."[10] The almost proverbial dictum, "There is but one step from the sublime to the ridiculous," is said to be a part of a soliloquy delivered by Napoleon on his return from Russia. Dr. H. Schlag denies that soliloquies are unnatural and insists that many persons when alone allow their thoughts to become audible.[11]

---

[1] Titan, 94. *Zykel,* Hempel's ed., Vol. 15–18, p. 434. For this and a few other quotations I am indebted to R. Franz, *ut supra.*

[2] Der grüne Heinrich, I, 44, ed. 1904.

[3] Merlin, I, 59, ed. 1892.

[4] Ein sanftes Weib, Magazin für Litteratur, 1897, p. 1506.

[5] *Op. cit.,* p. 868.

[6] Oeuvres complètes, ed. by Assezat, Paris, 1895. Belles Lettres IV, Chap. XVII.

[7] Oeuvres, second ed., Paris, 1767, Vol. I, p. 359 ff.

[8] Abhandlung vom Trauerspiele, in Bibliothek der schönen Wissenschaften, etc., 1757, I, p. 48 ff.

[9] *Op. cit.,* p. 433.

[10] Dramatik, Berlin, 1892, p. 169.

[11] Das Drama, Essen, 1909, p. 306 ff.

So much for the views, favorable and otherwise, on the soliloquy off the stage. What, on the other hand, are the views of the critics with regard to the dramatic soliloquy, the monolog? Long soliloquies have been the subject of attacks for several centuries and in many climes. About the middle of the 16th century an Italian critic, dramatist and impresario, De Sommi of Mantua, objects to monologs, basing his objection on the fact that long soliloquies on the street are entirely unnatural.[1] A reporter in Pesaro in 1574 bewails his sad lot, as the monotony of the soliloquies in a comedy he had to criticize proved almost unendurable.[2] Hédelin, Abbé d'Aubignac, (1657) objects strenuously to expositional soliloquies, *ce mauvais artifice, ce sécours étranger,* and also to emotional soliloquies whose position in the drama makes them absurd: as, e. g., when a lover, hearing of a danger that threatens his mistress, soliloquizes at great length instead of hurrying to her aid.[3] The Earl of Mulgrave in his "Essay on Poetry" (1717) believed that:

> "First then, Soliloquies had need be few,
> Extremely short, and spoke in passion too."[4]

Gottsched, a few years later (1730), after condemning all soliloquies on the ground that "kluge Leute pflegen nicht laut zu reden, wenn sie allein sind," relents and adds: "es wäre denn in besonderen Affekten, und das zwar mit wenig Worten."[5] Ramler, who is little more than the editor and translator of Batteux, insists that "every soliloquy must be short, because it is almost unnatural. If it is long, the person must be violently agitated."[6]

J. von Sonnenfels, theatrical censor at Vienna and author of "Briefe über die Wienerische Schaubühne," objects to all monologs on the ground of their improbability, especially to

---

[1] Geschichte des neueren Dramas, W. Creizenach, Vol. II, p. 287.

[2] *Ibid.,* note 2, p. 287.

[3] Pratique du Théâtre, Paris, 1657. Englished in 1684: The Whole Art of the Stage.

[4] An Essay on Poetry, London, 1717, p. 308.

[5] Versuch einer critischen Dichtkunst, p. 598.

[6] Einleitung in die schönen Wissenschaften, S. K. W. Ramler, Vol. II, p. 246 ff.

the purely expositional type. He finds them permissible only when passion is at its height, and the heart too small to contain the inner struggle. But even then long, logically arranged speeches are out of place. " In such moments the restless character utters disjointed, disconnected speeches, he articulates *gebrochene Töne,* he is restless, sits, stands, runs back and forth, acts strangely."[1] G. Freytag practically condemns dramatic soliloquies, saying that the isolation of a character on the stage always requires an apology, and that monologs are not a necessary adjunct of modern dramas because of the numerous opportunities of disclosing thoughts and feelings which the modern stage gives to the characters. He also claims that the art of acting has brought about a changed conception of dramatic effects.[2] Edgar Allan Poe finds both asides and soliloquies preposterous and not as respectable as the shifts employed by Chinese playwrights.[3] Henderson does not go quite so far as Freytag when he says: " Dramatic craftsmanship has to-day reached a point of such complex excellence that the best dramatists refuse to employ so unworthy a device as the lengthy soliloquy."[4] Brevity is also insisted upon by Mr. Archer: " A few broken exclamations under high emotion is all the soliloquy that strict art should permit, for high emotion does in many cases manifest itself in speech."[5] It is noteworthy that critics have been unanimous in condemning the expositional soliloquy.

Not all critics, however, have objected to the long dramatic soliloquy which lays bare the soul. ^Hédelin approved of it, though with misgivings, when he said: " I confess that it is sometimes very pleasant to see a man upon the stage lay open his heart, and speak boldly of his most secret thoughts, explain his designs, and give vent to all that his passion suggests; but without doubt it is very hard to make an actor do it

[1] Friedrich Düsel, Der dramatische Monolog in der Poetik des 17. und 18. Jahrhunderts und in den Dramen Lessings, p. 15, Hamburg, 1897.

[2] Technik des Dramas, 10th ed., 1905, p. 192 ff.

[3] Woodberry ed., Vol. 7, Marginalia.

[4] *Op. cit.,* p. 440.

[5] English Dramatists of Today, p. 274.

with probability."[1]   Diderot favors the emotional soliloquy, but objects to its being lengthy. Dr. Arnold's quotation: " Man speaks to himself only in moments of perplexity,"[2] is incomplete, as Diderot adds: " If long, it sins against the nature of dramatic action, which it holds in suspense too much."[3] Nicolai prefers the emotional monolog to a colorless conversation with a confidant.[4] Mendelssohn is especially enthusiastic about that type of soliloquy in which violent inner conflict precedes a final decision, but demands natural artless expression in all emotional soliloquies.[5] Though Freytag in his authoritative dramaturgic work is rather unfriendly to the soliloquy, he is willing to tolerate the introspective soliloquy, provided that it has dramatic structure and direct bearing upon the action. He insists that it must contain " Satz, Gegensatz, Ergebnis und zwar Schlussergebnis, das für die Handlung selbst Bedeutung gewinnt."[6] J. J. Engel made the same demand as early as 1774: " The monolog must be really dramatic—monologs which bring about an important change in the frame of mind of the character, and by that means in the plot, are commendable."[7]

Lessing,[8] following in Diderot's footsteps, is a warm admirer of the emotional soliloquy. A. W. von Schlegel demands that every emotional soliloquy be cast in the dialog form, that it be *sich mit sich selbst besprechen*,[9] as though the character were divided into two persons. Hebbel insists upon the same characteristic: " Monologs are only proper when there is dualism in the individual, so that the two persons who at other times ought to be on the stage seem to be active in his breast."[10] According to Hegel[11] all introspective soliloquies are justified,

---

[1] The Whole Art of the Stage, p. 57.

[2] P. 18.

[3] Oeuvres complètes, Paris, 1875; Belles Lettres IV, Chap. XVII.

[4] F. Nicolai, Abhandlung vom Trauerspiele, Bibliothek der schönen Wissenschaften und der freyen Künste, Vol. I, p. 48.

[5] Gesammelte Schriften, 1843, Vol. I, p. 321 ff.

[6] Technik des Dramas, p. 192 ff.

[7] Schriften, 1802, Vol. 4, p. 228. For this and a few other citations I am indebted to the scholarly monograph of F. Düsel.

[8] Hamburgische Dramaturgie, 48. Stück.

[9] Sämmtliche Werke, Leipzig, 1846, VII, 50.

[10] Tagebücher, II, 2971, ed. by Werner, Berlin, 1904.

[11] Aesthetik, Vol. III. Quoted by R. v. Gottschall in Zur Kritik des modernen Dramas, Berlin, 1900, Chap. on Der Monolog im Drama. p. 112.

whether they are calmly reflective or rent by inner conflict. Vischer,[1] on the other hand, demands *Affekt* i. e. emotion. Among other admirers I might mention Mundt,[2] Gartelmann,[3] Schlag,[4] Gottschall,[5] Ludwig,[6] Delius,[7] Kilian.[7]

Contemporary opinion as mirrored in the modern naturalistic dramas appears distinctly hostile to the dramatic soliloquy, this hostility manifesting itself in ostracizing the once welcome assistant. Gottschall, an ardent admirer of the soliloquy, sums up the present condition as follows: "From the Berlin Sinai ten new commandments are announced to the kneeling populace. And to these ten belongs the following: Thou shalt no longer write monologs!"[8] But this new state of affairs is not without precedents. As Dr. Arnold points out, Corneille, more than two centuries ago, discarded the soliloquy in the greater part of his later works and comments upon the fact in the introduction to his works, thus showing that it was premeditated and not accidental.[9] Molière's masterpieces also contain practically no soliloquies, his "Impromptu," the "Critique" and the "Comtesse d'Escarbagnnes" having none at all. German literature furnishes us a precedent in the dramas of the pupils and followers of Gottsched, especially those of Johann Elias Schlegel and Frau Gottsched. Gottsched's "Deutsche Schaubühne"[10] consists for the greater part of plays in which soliloquies and asides are entirely avoided.[11] Why did their departure from traditional dramatic technic fail to influence succeeding dramatists? Why could they not exert the same influence that Ibsen through his technic has exerted upon the playwrights of practically every modern language? Pri-

---

[1] Aesthetik, Stuttgart, 1857, Vol. IV, p. 1392.
[2] Theodor Mundt, Dramaturgie, Berlin, 1848, p. 138 ff.
[3] Dramatik, Berlin, 1892, p. 169 ff.
[4] Das Drama, p. 306 ff.
[5] Zur Kritik des modernen Dramas, Berlin, 1900, pp. 109–127.
[6] Otto Ludwig, Shakespeare-Studien, ed. by M. Heydrich, 1874, Nachlassschriften, Vol. II, p. 105.
[7] Arnold, p. 19.
[8] *Op. cit.,* p. 109.
[9] Arnold, p. 15.
[10] Leipzig, 1740–1745.
[11] Rudolf Franz, Der Monolog und Ibsen, p. 32.

marily and chiefly because contemporary and succeeding dramatists (and incidentally audiences) did not question the convention of the soliloquy. Then, too, the small intrinsic worth of the plays militated against their being used as models by other dramatists. For some years past, however, the dramatic soliloquy has been subjected to criticism, which received added stimulus from the new technic of Ibsen's powerful plays. But when a convention is attacked and becomes the topic of dispute, its days are numbered. As Paull so aptly expresses it: "A convention that is questioned is doomed; its existence depends upon its unhesitating acceptance."[1]

The drama has its conventions as well as every other art. A convention is an implied pact between the artist and his patrons to accept certain variations from real life as absolutely essential means of expression.[2] To enjoy an opera we must accept the convention that all the characters express themselves through the medium of song; in sculpture we do not look for color (although Klinger has favored the world of art with a few colored statues); in paintings motion is out of the question. Dramatic convention, then, is an agreement between the author and the public, between those before the curtain and those behind it, to accept variations from real life off the stage as a part of the game. Among the conventions of the drama some are essential, and these may be termed permanent because of their enduring qualities. Others, however, have changed from age to age; after being used for a time they have been discarded, and these might be called temporary conventions. Among the permanent conventions are the removal of the fourth wall of the room so that we can see what is taking place, the raising of the actors' voices so that we can hear them, the elucidation of the plot so that we can follow it, making the action much more compact than it would be in life, the condensation of the dialog, as we have only a short time in the theater. Some of the temporary conventions are the use of prose, verse, rime, assonance and the soliloquy. The latter has been so tenacious a convention, that one might well say that it has been

---

1 Fortnightly Review, May, 1899, p. 870.
2 Brander Matthews, The Development of the Drama, p. 2 ff.

demoted to the temporary division after being at home in the other division for centuries.

The dramatic soliloquy, then, is a convention and is not based on real life. As generally stated, this variation from life, this convention, permits an actor who believes himself to be alone on the stage to make his thoughts audible so that the audience hears them and becomes acquainted with what would otherwise be unknown to them. In other words, "an actor soliloquizing must be supposed to be thinking aloud."[1] Does this statement regarding the underlying principle of the monolog cover the ground and include all types? It would seem that only the introspective soliloquies, those that reveal thought and feeling, are taken care of. The expositional soliloquy, which conveys information regarding the plot or the characters to the audience, is not provided for in that definition. I should formulate the principle underlying the expositional soliloquy as follows: The speaker loses his personality for the time being, becomes the mouthpiece of the author, and, while talking to himself (in reality to the audience), conveys to the audience such information as the author desires; whereas the introspective monolog is highly subjective and vibrant with the speaker's personality, the expositional type is colorless, objective and impersonal.

Given the problem of reducing the dramatic soliloquy to its lowest terms, the investigator would doubtless find the result to be, broadly speaking, the soliloquy conveying information and the soliloquy revealing thought and emotion. Classified according to their underlying convention, the former might be termed verbal soliloquy, the latter a thought soliloquy. Lastly, their relation to the audience differs, inasmuch as the soliloquy conveying information always implies a consciousness of the audience, especially so in its crude use in early German drama, while the thought soliloquy never implies a knowledge of the spectators.

The soliloquy that imparts information has played a most important rôle in the construction of the drama, especially at the beginning, where it performs the important office of putting

[1] Brander Matthews, Concerning the Soliloquy, Putnam's Monthly, Nov., 1906.

the audience in touch with the author, of bridging over the chasm between author and spectator. The spectators, in order to understand the action, must be made aware of certain facts concerning the characters and the plot; they must become acquainted with certain events that have occurred before the play begins. The task of conveying such information, known as exposition, may be undertaken by monolog or dialog. The former is a labor saving device, fulfilling its task with ease and despatch, but critics from Hédelin down to the present time have pronounced it crude, unnatural, a lame makeshift, an insult to the intelligence of the audience. The latter, on the other hand, though slower and more difficult, is the more artistic method. The expositional soliloquy was a favorite device with German dramatists before Hauptmann, Holz, Sudermann, and other members of the modern naturalistic school, not only at the beginning of the play but throughout its course. In a play the author is often confronted with the necessity of imparting some specific piece of information to the audience in order to prevent confusion, and without compunction he resorts to the least taxing and simplest method, viz., the expositional soliloquy. It may describe some event: a battle, a murder, or what not, that has occurred off the stage during the progress of the play or is occurring back of the scenes; it may be narrative, identifying, self-characterizing, or it may be employed to reveal the plans and intentions of the speaker. No matter when explanation is necessary, the expositional soliloquy is ready and willing to jump into the breach. The different types of expositional soliloquy may be classified as follows: 1. introductory exposition, 2. identification, 3. self-characterization, 4. narration, 5. description, 6. intention.

Naturally the purest and least adulterated forms of the expositional soliloquy are found among the early dramatists, the authors of church plays, Hans Sachs, and his contemporaries, handicapped as they were by a very crude technic and but a step removed from the epic style. To be sure we find examples of the baldly expositional soliloquy throughout German dramatic literature (except in the naturalistic drama of today, as previously stated), but generally some attempt is made to render it more plausible by giving it an emotional admixture or an individual touch.

The introductory expositional soliloquy supplies the audience with such information regarding the plot and the characters as is necessary for following the story intelligently. Before Gryphius the majority of plays began with this short cut; beginning with him, however, the dialog opening was the preferred method of attack. We find introductory expositional soliloquies in two of Gryphius's plays, "Carolus Stuardus" and "Papinianus," in Lessing's "Philotas" and "Emilia Galotti," in Schiller's prolog to "Die Jungfrau von Orleans," in Goethe's "Iphigenie" and in his "Faust," although there is a large admixture of other elements in both the latter, in Grillparzer s "Ahnfrau," "Des Meeres und der Liebe Wellen," and "Der Traum ein Leben," in Hebbel's "Michelangelo" and "Agnes Bernauer." More than forty of Sach's shrovetide plays and many of his comedies and tragedies furnish uncontaminated examples of this type.

The soliloquy employed to identify the speaker generally occurs at the beginning of the play, but it is not confined to that position. The church plays furnish numerous examples: "I am Abel, who was murdered by his brother"—"I am Isaiah, one of the prophets."[1] The shrovetide plays of the fifteenth century, Hans Sachs, and many others, use this same naïve type: "I am called Mr. Tannheuser, my name is known far and wide," "I am called Eulenspiegel and am known throughout Germany."[2] In Iphigenie's opening speech Goethe makes use of this type, yet with what a world of consummate skill!

The self-characterizing type is an outgrowth of the previous type and is often added to it. After the speaker has told his name, he goes on to give a frank recital of his characteristics. So, e. g., Eulenspiegel, after introducing himself, proceeds to discuss his innate knavery and to illustrate it. We find this type in classical and nineteenth century drama, but there it has been raised to a higher plane. The villain makes use of it to disclose his real vicious self, e. g., Franz Moor in "Die Räu-

[1] Redentiner Osterspiel, ed. by T. Froning, pp. 133, 134.
[2] Hans Sachs, Fastnachtspiele.

ber," Marwood in "Miss Sara Sampson," Adelheid in "Götz," Zawish in "König Ottokars Glück und Ende." Occasionally, however, a frank bit of self-characterization is met with; Siegfried indulging in it in Hebbel's "Genoveva."[1] A more highly developed technic allows the audience to draw its own conclusions as to the actor's character, which displays itself both in dialog and in soliloquies of an introspective nature.

Descriptive and narrative soliloquies occur in such numbers in the early period that they make the plays fairly topheavy. Nor are they infrequent in the later plays. A good example of the soliloquy which describes events that are going on simultaneously off the stage occurs in "Emilia Galotti,"[2] when Marinelli stands at the window and keeps the audience posted as to what is going on outside. There is one instance even in Hauptmann, Rektor Besenmeyer repeating part of the service in the adjoining church.[3] Ordinary descriptive and narrative soliloquies that contain only a bald recital of facts are not frequent, but almost every dramatist contributes one or more examples. In "Minna von Barnhelm" Werner delivers a soliloquy which is filled with frankly narrative material,[4] in "Käthchen von Heilbronn" the Count[5] and the Emperor[6] deliver narrative speeches. Eugenie's speech in "Die natürliche Tochter" will illustrate the descriptive type.[7]

The soliloquy that explains the plans and intentions of the speaker may be either complete in itself, or it may be merely an appendage of another soliloquy, usually of the narrative type. Werner's previously quoted speech ends in this manner, as do several soliloquies in "Götz."[8] Franz Moor's diabolical soliloquy at the beginning of Act 2 is a splendid example of how this type can be infused with dramatic life, by showing us the mental processes which led up to the formulation of the

---

[1] Act I, Sc. 1, end.
[2] Act, 3, Sc. 2. Also Lessing: Nathan, Act II, Sc. 1, beginning.
[3] Florian Geyer, Act 3, p. 47.
[4] Act III, Sc. 6, entire.
[5] Act IV, Sc. 2.
[6] Act V, Sc. 2.
[7] Act V, Sc. 6.
[8] Act 1, Sc. 2; Act I, end.

plan. Even the simple statement of a plan is made highly effective when delivered under emotional stress, as in Ferdinand's speech in "Kabale und Liebe."[1]

The introspective soliloquy is the medium for expressing the thoughts and feelings of the actor. In contradistinction to its shiftless relative, the expositional soliloquy, which it is hard to defend, the introspective soliloquy might be termed the true soliloquy, as it makes known to us thoughts and emotions that would otherwise remain hidden. "It lets a tortured hero unpack his heart; it opens a window into his soul; and it gives the spectator a pleasure not to be had otherwise. It allows us to listen to the communing of a character with himself, as though we were not overhearing what he is saying."[2]

The thought soliloquy may be subdivided into reflective, moralizing, and deliberative. The emotional soliloquy may express any one of the emotions as anger, fear, love, hate, joy, grief, despair, shame, jealousy, revenge, longing, contempt, disgust, irritation.

In the reflective soliloquy the speaker's thought is turned back upon past experiences or ideas and his attitude toward them made clear. Tell's famous soliloquy[3] before he murders Gessler splendidly illustrates this type. It usually occurs at the conclusion of a dialog when the actor who is alone on the stage reverts to the matters just touched upon in the conversation and acquaints the audience with the thought or thoughts uppermost in his mind, in other words, his mental reaction. So Pylades, after his conversation with Iphigenie, Act 2, Sc. 2: "She seemed greatly moved by the fate of the royal house. Whoever she may be, she has known the king well, and fortunately for us, has been sold to this place from a noble family. Be quiet, dear heart, and let us steer courageously toward the star of hope that shines for us." Lessing's dramas show a fondness for this type, several examples occurring in almost every play.

The moralizing soliloquy goes a step further than the reflective, as it indulges in moral reflections and draws practical les-

1 Act I, end.
2 Brander Matthews, A Study of the Drama, p. 149.
3 Act 4, Sc. 3.

sons from past experiences, thus introducing a conscious didactic strain. The early plays from the serious dramas of Sachs through the dramas of the reformation have a large admixture of this moralizing element. Virtue and vice, right and wrong, are the pegs upon which these little sermons are hung. In the philosophical soliloquy a wider field is drawn upon, abstract ideas rather than the concrete are at the basis of the musing. Faust's immortal reveries, Primislaus in "Libussa,"[1] Wallenstein on custom,[2] Sappho's beautiful outbursts,[3] Attinghausen on the passing of the good old days,[4]—these are some of the splendid examples that can be found in German literature.

The deliberative soliloquy considers and examines the reasons for and against a proposition, it estimates the weight and force of arguments, it views the probable consequences of an action in order to reach a decision. Nathan's soliloquy[5] just prior to his interview with Saladin, and Posa's speech[6] in a similar situation show this calm examination of the pros and cons. Very often, however, there is a considerable admixture of emotion in this type, and in that case the speaker reveals an inner conflict. Where thought is subordinated to, and outweighed by, feeling the soliloquy will be referred to as a conflict soliloquy. Odoardo's soliloquy, Act 5, Sc. 4,[7] not only illustrates the subordination of thought to passion, but calls attention to it: "Aber sieh da! Schon wieder; schon wieder rennet der Zorn mit dem Verstande davon"—and then begins to examine the possibilities calmly. Other examples are Moor's "to be or not to be,"[8] Fiesco's soliloquies in the second[9] and third acts,[10] Philotas's outburst in the fourth scene,[11] the soliloquy of the Tempelherr, Act 5, Sc. 3.[12]

[1] Act III, Sc. 1.
[2] Wallenstein's Tod, Act I, Sc. 4.
[3] Act III, Sc. 1. Act IV, Sc. 1.
[4] Wilhelm Tell, Act II, Sc. 1.
[5] Act III, Sc. 6, in Nathan der Weise.
[6] Don Carlos, Act III, Sc. 9.
[7] Emilia Galotti.
[8] Die Räuber, Act IV, Sc. 5.
[9] Act II, Sc. 19.
[10] Act III, Sc. 2.
[11] Wilhelm Tell, Act II, Sc. 1.
[12] Nathan der Weise.

As the term "emotional soliloquy" is not subject to misinterpretation, and as even one example for each of the numerous emotions would take up altogether too much space, further discussion is not necessary.

It is a generally accepted theory that the stage, architecturally speaking, has exerted an unmistakable influence upon the drama.[1] In other words, the form of the stage of a certain period has to a large extent determined the form of the play. The soliloquy is an example of this influence, as the close proximity of the spectators to the actors on the stage of the early epochs produced an atmosphere of intimacy which made the expositional soliloquy seem perfectly in place. The stage of today, set apart from the audience and supplied with remarkable scenic and lighting effects, produces such an air of naturalness, of vraisemblance, that the expositional speech seems altogether out of place. The lack of stage settings in the earliest period and poor illumination later on, made explanation of "business" on the stage necessary. Many actions on the stage would have been unintelligible to the spectators had not the actor explained what he was doing. To illustrate: in Sachs's shrovetide play "The Peasant in Purgatory," the farmer, after being drugged, is to be thrown into a dark cell. Another actor carries him on the stage, lays him down and announces that the farmer is now in the cell. Immediately after that the peasant according to stage directions "clears his throat, gets up and gropes about in all directions." Without an explanation the spectators would have difficulty in interpreting his actions and visualizing the scene, therefore an explanatory soliloquy is delivered by the peasant: "Hang it, where am I? What a dark hole this is! I see and hear nothing here. I take hold of nothing but four stone walls," etc. In the last analysis, of course, all soliloquies of this type are expositional, as they convey information to the audience.

The structural soliloquy, on the other hand, is primarily a mechanical device whose function it is to prevent friction in the wheelwork of the drama, a lubricant as it were. One vari-

---

[1] Freytag, Technik des Dramas, 10th ed., p. 160.

3

ety of the structural soliloquy is referred to by Düsel[1] as the *Pausenfüllmonolog,* which is employed to fill a gap between the exit of one player and the entrance of another. Dr. Arnold refers to this as the link soliloquy, and adds two other varieties: the entrance and exit soliloquy. The entrance soliloquy "prevents the simultaneous appearance of A at one door and B at the other. Even though they were meeting by appointment, they probably would not arrive at the same instant. So A comes on a moment before B, and fills the interval with some remark."[2] The exit soliloquy was used at the end of an act to prevent the awkwardness resulting from several people leaving the stage at the same time. One accordingly remained behind and delivered a short speech. The drop curtain of course made these two types unnecessary, as it may rise or fall on an assembled group. Both the entrance and exit soliloquy are infrequent in German drama, as the early playwrights had no compunctions about allowing two or more characters to enter and leave simultaneously. In Sachs, e. g., the stereotyped stage direction at the end of the act is, "they both depart, or they all depart." At the beginning of an act we find either an expositional soliloquy or the simultaneous entrance of two or more characters. In the plays of Heinrich Julius there are a few examples of entrance and exit soliloquy, e. g., in " Buhler und Buhlerin," II, 2; II, 5; IV, 7, but even in these there is an admixture of the expositional element. The unwillingness to have the stage empty or to have a pause between the exit of one actor and the entrance of another is responsible for the link soliloquy. Lessing was fond of this device, especially in his early plays, as Düsel points out. In his plays the form is rather stereotyped: a brief reference to what has preceded followed by an announcement of the approach of a character—ha, there he is!

The link soliloquy as such is shortlived. Lessing in his later plays and succeeding dramatists transformed the structural device into an integral part of the play by making it the vehicle

---

1 *Op. cit.,* pp. 22–25, 42.
2 *Op. cit.,* p. 81.

for reflections on the preceding scene, i. e., a reflective or thought soliloquy.

After the preceding classification and definitions, just a word as to the scope and purpose of this investigation. It will be in the main a portrayal of the career of a dramatic convention, the soliloquy, as manifested in German drama from its infancy, i. e., the church plays, to the present time. Although principally a historical study, the investigation will attempt to throw light on the question whether the recent drama has, or has not, gained in artistic effectiveness by its gradual disuse of the soliloquy. Two questions then will be answered: 1. What rôle does the soliloquy play in the technic of the various German dramatists? 2. Is dramatic technic improved by the elimination of the soliloquy?

CHAPTER I

Early Indigenous Drama

1. *Medieval Church Plays*

Moralizing embodied in a dramatic spectacle is less odious and vastly more effective than a sermon from a pulpit. Realizing this, the priests fostered the different types of religious drama which had their origin in the various church festivals. The germs of the Easter play, e. g., are found in the Catholic ritual and consist of four sentences that are chanted by two semi-choruses representing the three Marys who visit Christ's tomb and the angels who tell them that Christ has risen. These sentences form the basis of the Latin Easter play, which in turn gave rise to a Latin-German form, in which the Latin speeches were translated into German for the benefit of the uneducated spectators, and finally resulted in plays that were almost entirely German. The last mentioned gave rise to the unwieldy passion plays, which sometimes lasted three to four days and required several hundred actors.[1]

The plays were at first performed in the church, but as they grew to such dimensions that the church could no longer accommodate them, they were taken to an open air stage that was usually set up in the market place. The stage[2] was a large wooden platform, somewhat longer than it was wide, which was not raised far from the ground, so that all parts of it were visible to the standing or sitting spectators. It represented all the places which were necessary in the action, such as houses, gardens, cities, castles, etc. Naturally, these are only indicated, and that in the crudest manner, so that even in the fifteenth century the top of a mountain, the roof of the temple and hell were all represented by a barrel. The actors were visible throughout the entire play. At the beginning of

[1] R. Froning, Das Drama des Mittelalters, in 3 vols., Vol. I, p. 4.
[2] *Ibid.*, Vol. I, p. 266 ff.

the play, or rather just previous to the opening, the actors march upon the stage in solemn procession and sit down in their appointed places, which they leave only when the play requires their presence elsewhere.

The dramatic art was as crude as the stage and its settings. The whole treatment was epic rather than dramatic and the author's main concern was to get the story across. Selection of essentials, compression of the plot or dialog did not trouble the playwrights, as they believed in describing everything in the greatest detail.

In one respect the author of a church play was decidedly better off than later playwrights: there was no need of introductory exposition as his audience was familiar with biblical lore. The only difficulty he faced was to let the audience know who the characters were that appeared in the play. This he did in the least taxing manner by having every character about whom there was any doubt simply tell the spectators who he was, in other words, by employing the identifying soliloquy. To be sure this is an elastic use of the term, for, strictly speaking, these speeches are addressed directly to the audience and therefore are not soliloquies. This also applies to the narrative soliloquies of which there are a few examples,[1] and to those expressing the speaker's intention. Illustrations of the identifying soliloquy are numerous: "Redentiner Osterspiel," 260 ff., 685 ff.; "Wiener Passionsspiel," 65 ff.; "Alsfelder Passionspiel," 7189 ff.; and in every "Krämerscene" the different characters are introduced in this manner. Occasionally a bit of self-characterization is added as in the "Alsfelder" play, 1253 ff. The Redentin play has two good examples of the intentional speech: 250 ff. where Jesus tells of his plan to go to hell and release Adam and Eve and the holy fathers, and 1950 ff. where Lucifer discloses his plan of catching all sinners and bringing them to hell.

Real emotional soliloquies, however, do occur, although not in great numbers. The type in which the speaker is so overcome with emotion that he is entirely oblivious of his surroundings is on the whole more frequent than the type in

[1] Trierer Osterspiel, 161–5, Vol. I, p. 55. Alsfelder Passionsspiel, 3622–27, Vol. 3, p. 701.

which the speaker is alone. Those who object that a character can not be alone as all the actors are on the stage must remember that the action moves from place to place and that any one² station with its group of actors constitutes the stage for the time being and the remainder becomes non-existent. So, when Peter in the "Frankfurter Passionssspiel," after denying that he knows Christ, leaves the house to deliver a soliloquy of remorse,¹ that part of the platform for the time being becomes an empty stage and he is alone on the stage. The same applies to Judas, who delivers a stirring soliloquy of remorse² while going away to commit suicide. The stage directions read: " Judas throws the coins on the ground and goes out to hang himself, saying on the way etc." Neither one of these soliloquies implies the least consciousness of the audience and are accordingly real soliloquies. In the "Alsfelder Passionsspiel" Peter is also alone when delivering his soliloquy of remorse,³ as the stage directions read: "Peter leaves weeping bitterly and withdraws from Christ and says." The speech, however, is not as effective as in the Frankfurt play. Judas's speech of remorse⁴ in the Alsfeld play on the other hand is weakened by being partly addressed to the audience: "O friends, now hear my complaint, which I am about to indulge in! I was one of the twelve apostles; I have betrayed my lord and master and sold him to the Jews! Therefore I shall now commit suicide,"⁴—then he begins his lament as follows: "Oh God that I was ever born," etc. But for the introduction it would be a true soliloquy. Every "Marienklage" illustrates the type of emotional soliloquy, which shows the speaker entirely oblivious to his surroundings. Other examples are Mary Magdalen's soliloquies of remorse and regret in the Frankfurt⁵ and Alsfeld plays,⁶ Lucifer's soliloquy of anxiety⁷ at Satan's long absence in the Redentin play, and his outburst of remorse⁸ later in the same play.

1 2614 ff.
2 2650 ff.
3 3594 ff.
4 3622 ff.
5 1076 ff.
6 1994 ff.
7 1691 ff.
8 1928 ff.

Grief, regret and remorse are the emotions most often represented in the soliloquies. There is one splendid example of the gloating villain in the Alsfeld play,[1] where Satan, after causing the death of the Baptist, steps forth and shouts: "Oho, oho! I have seen that my wish has been carried out: the man has been murdered though innocent." The thought soliloquy does not occur independently, but occasionally as a part of another type. In one of Lucifer's soliloquies of remorse this bit of moralizing is incorporated: "This is the result of pride! Pride is the beginning of all sin, pride has lowered us devils to the abyss."[2] At rare intervals there is also a reflective bit very much in the nature of an aside, e. g., in the Frankfurt play after Christ has spoken a few lines of Latin, Lieberman Rabi says: "We are all surprised that Christ can speak Latin, although he never attended school! It strikes me that that is not proper."[3]

The soliloquy which explains "business" or actions on the stage is not pressed into service very often, as most of the actions are perfectly intelligible to the spectators. Additional precautions are taken by having a person not in the play interrupt it occasionally and tell the audience just what scene will be presented next, together with its contents, e. g., Augustinus in the Frankfurt play. In unusual cases explanation becomes necessary, as when Lucifer looks for Christ's soul after the death on the cross,[4] and when the earth quakes after Christ's death.[5] The peculiar part of the latter description is that it begins in the present tense and after one sentence continues in the past tense as though the speaker were quoting some one else.

2. Shrovetide Plays of the 15th Century[6]

German secular drama has its origin in the carnival mummeries which were a popular form of amusement during the

---

[1] 1040 ff.
[2] Redentin play, 1946 ff.
[3] 850 ff.
[4] 4151 ff.
[5] 4156 ff.
[6] Fastnachtspiele aus dem 15. Jahrhundert, a collection of 121 plays ed. by Dr. Keller, Stuttgart, 1853.

few days before Lent with its long period of enforced sobriety. Throngs of masked citizens paraded through the cities and entered private residences, inns and bar-rooms, where they sought to evoke laughter by mimicking certain types that embodied ludicrous characteristics. Mimicry was soon supplemented by the spoken word, and the boorish peasant, the arrogant knight, the immoral priest and others are held up to ridicule in satiric speeches. The crudest type consists of a series of identifying and self-characterizing speeches. The masked actors enter together, each delivers a self-characterizing speech and they depart after being dined and wined. Then there are court scenes in which cases of every description are tried in a farcical manner, usually complaints against unfaithful husbands, which, however, did not result in divorces. Doctor scenes are also quite common in which a quack, after boasting of his skill and his marvellous cures, gives the patient some ludicrous prescription. Everyday life furnishes most of the themes but serious matters dealing with religious and social conditions are not tabooed. In fact it is sometimes difficult to tell where the religious play ends and the carnival play begins, as the latter has encroached so far upon the domain of the former.[1]

Very few of the shrovetide plays were performed on the stage, or rather platform, such as was used for church plays. Froning states that the more serious plays such as Nos. 111 and 119 in Keller required a stage. All others got along without stage or scenery, as they were repeated in places where such things were out of the question. The prolog of the first play in Keller throws an interesting light upon the average place of performance and the simple preparations.

Real soliloquies do not occur in these plays, although we might term the identifying, self-characterizing, narrative and descriptive speeches crude expositional soliloquies. Some of the plays in which there is a crude plot are developed entirely by means of dialog: Nos. 22, 37, 111. The last named deals with the legend of Pope Joan and is a good example of the

---

[1] Froning, Vol. 3, pp. 955 ff.; E. Devrient, Geschichte der deutschen Schauspielkunst, 1848, Vol. I, p. 96 ff.

blending of religious and secular drama. Gottsched calls it " das älteste tragische gedruckte deutsche Originalstück."[1] In No. 57, entitled " Ain guot Vasnachtspil " there are three asides in the dialog, possibly the earliest use of this device.

3. *Drama of the Reformation*

Almost everywhere the medieval church drama was put to utter rout by the Reformation, first because the Protestants objected to it as a Catholic institution, and secondly because the times were too stormy to permit people to sit calmly and enjoy the epic meanderings of the church plays. The drama that took its place was used principally as a weapon of attack and defense, especially by the Protestants, against religious adversaries. Epic treatment and endless sermonizing coupled with the exposition of the Lutheran doctrine characterize these plays. The stage and the scenery was crude and virtually that of the church plays, and the plays were given in churches, schools and public squares.

Some of the plays, such as " Die Totenfresser "[2] by Gengenbach, required no stage or setting and were probably performed on the street. Gengenbach occupied a unique position in the drama of this period, as he began in the Catholic camp and ended as a rabid champion of the Reformation. His " Zehn Alter dieser Welt "[3] is permeated by the Catholic doctrine, while the " Totenfresser " is a bitter attack upon the practice of giving masses for the souls of the departed. The gist of the latter is that the only ones that benefit by these masses are the pope and the clergy, who are able to live in luxurious ease from the proceeds. The play is utterly undramatic and is to all intents and purposes a series of expositional soliloquies which set forth the views of the adherents and opponents of the Catholic church.

" Der Ablasskrämer "[4] is not much more dramatic and con-

---

[1] Vol. II, p. 82, quoted by Keller.

[2] Das Drama der Reformationszeit, ed. by R. Froning, Stuttgart, pp. 3–10, date 1525.

[3] In Keller: Fastnachtspiele des 15. Jahrhunderts.

[4] Froning, p. 13 ff., date, 1525.

sists of a series of denunciations hurled at the salesman by those whom he has formerly duped. Oratorical attacks are supplemented by physical assaults and the vender is compelled to admit all his shameful practices. A reflective soliloquy near the end of the play shows him a sadder but wiser man.

"Der verlorene Sohn"[1] by Waldis is the oldest Protestant drama based upon a biblical theme and paved the way for a host of imitations, the prodigal son soon becoming a favorite theme with dramatists. Besides being a "Tendenzdrama" it has a special point of interest in the fact that it is the first German drama that shows influences of the Roman drama by the division into acts, the introduction of riotous scenes with the meretrices and the deceptive innkeeper. The introductory expositional soliloquy is addressed to the audience, the other expositional speeches avoid this crudity. Several asides by the innkeeper as he plucks the prodigal possibly show Latin influence. There is but one emotional soliloquy, an outburst of sorrowful regret by the prodigal after he has been plucked.

"Susanna"[2] by Rebhuhn is the earliest German play that shows "a conscious striving for artistic effects of poetic form and dramatic construction."[3] The play is divided into five acts and has a prolog, epilog and chorus at the end of the first four acts. Of all the Susanna plays this is the best and the most effective, as it is the simplest. A long expositional soliloquy which reveals the villainy of a rich rascal and the corruptness of the judges is interesting, as it is introduced solely to characterize the venality of the bench. On the whole then the technic of the soliloquy in these plays is on the same level as in the church plays.

4. Hans Sachs

The early shrovetide plays of Sachs were undoubtedly presented in inns and private homes, as were those of the 15th century, and probably the same method of presentation prevailed. The later plays may possibly have been presented on the stage used for the larger plays, i. e., the so-called comedies

---

[1] Froning, p. 31 ff., date 1527.
[2] Froning, p. 101 ff., date 1536.
[3] Calvin Thomas, German Literature, p. 158.

and tragedies. The latter were performed for the most part in churches, the regular rendezvous of the mastersingers, on crude stages erected for this purpose.[1] But as early as 1550 the mastersingers built the first German theater in Nürnberg for the performance of larger plays, probably realizing the inappropriateness of giving them in churches.[2] Or it is possible that the clergy strenuously objected to such performances in the churches.

The form of the stage of this period is largely a matter of conjecture, although stage directions in the plays throw a little light upon the subject. Very likely then the stage consisted of a platform raised about three feet from the ground and open to the spectators on three sides. A broad partition about six feet high ran across the rear of the stage so as to form a dressing room and wings for the actors. There may have been a real door or merely a curtain through which the actors entered the stage from this enclosed space. The top of this subdivision was open so that the smoke of a conflagration off the stage was visible and the tumult of a battle plainly audible to the spectators; the sides, however, were probably covered so that changes in costume would not be seen.[1] In front of this main stage there was sometimes a lower stage, especially in the theaters upon which the mastersingers may have sung the entr'acte music.[2] There was no scenery or stage-setting of any sort, no curtain to mark the beginning or end of an act; the characters came out upon the stage at the beginning of an act and left it at the conclusion of the act.

Considering the simplicity of the stage and the ease with which one could be erected, it is supposable that the wealthy citizens often entertained their friends by giving theatricals in their homes.

The stereotyped form with which the comedies and tragedies begin is a prolog by the "ernholdt" or herald, who gives the audience a brief synopsis of the play followed by an introductory expositional soliloquy. The plays themselves are simply

[1] Anton Glock, Die Bühne des Hans Sachs, Passau, 1903.
[2] E. Devrient, Geschichte der deutschen Schauspielkunst, Vol. I, p. 113 ff.

stories cast in the dialog form; getting the story across is the main object of the author, who is not concerned with the struggle of one will against another, with the inner processes that give rise to a decision, with the soul-state resulting from a given act. As Freytag puts it: "Nicht die Darstellung einer Begebenheit an sich, sondern ihrer Einwirkung auf die Menschenseele ist Aufgabe der dramatischen Kunst."[1] The plays regularly conclude with a moralizing sermon which is also delivered by the herald.

Almost half of the shrovetide plays have neither prolog or epilog, and in most of the others the prolog has been reduced to a mere formula of greeting, generally: "ein guten abent ir erbarn leut." In the plays that have a prolog a dialog opening is usually employed. Occasionally, especially in the later plays, an expositional soliloquy follows the prolog in the manner of the tragedies and comedies.[2] When Sachs discards the more or less stereotyped prolog he decidedly favors the soliloquy as the vehicle for attack. In more than forty cases soliloquies are used, whereas a dialog opening occurs in only thirteen of the plays, notably in his later productions.[3]

In his later comedies and tragedies there is also a growing tendency to discard the opening soliloquy and employ dialog. In eight comedies written between 1556 and 1560 four have the dialog opening; in eight tragedies of the same period seven begin with dialog.

The introductory expositional soliloquies are generally frankly addressed to the audience, but there are numerous cases where the character is required by the stage directions to talk to himself or herself—"red mit im selb," or "red mit ir selb." The speech itself in this case is usually cast in the same mold as those addressed to the audience and is in no sense a talking to one's self. But there are instances where this expositional speech is raised to a higher artistic level by making it an apostrophe to Fortune, as in "Die schön Marina"—"Great praise and thanks to thee, O Fortune! How richly and abundantly

[1] G. Freytag, Die Technik des Dramas, Leipzig, 1905, p. 18.
[2] Fastnachtspiele, Nos. 68, 70, 71, 73.
[3] Ibid., Nos. 20, 25, 27, 35, 36, 43, 50, 59, 60, 61, 62, 80, 83.

thou hast provided me with everything so that no sorrow can approach me!" etc. To be sure, the speech gradually sinks to the level of frank exposition, but the attempt to get away from the direct address to the audience is praiseworthy. In "Fortunatus" we find an apostrophe to God in the opening soliloquy: "Oh God in heaven to thee I lament the fact that I spent my young days so foolishly," etc. In "Der teuffel mit dem kauffmann" the apostrophe to Fortune is carried through to the end of the speech, thus producing quite an artistic effect. An emotional admixture is occasionally used to good effect and absolves the soliloquy from the charge that it is addressed to the audience, e. g., in "Das böss weyb mit den worten etc. gut zu machen" and in "Die vier unglückhafften liebhabenden personen." In the former the henpecked husband says: "Alas, poor wretched man that I am, what shall I do? That which is given as a comfort to men troubles my life most. Oh! Oh! Oh! Oh! alas! alas! wherever I stand and go I have nothing but trouble which only the grave can free me from!"

The soliloquy used for identification, a crude makeshift which occurs so often in the church plays and in the shrovetide plays of the 15th century, is also employed by Sachs. Nor is its use confined to the early plays; on the contrary, it crops to the surface continually. In the earliest of the shrovetide plays, dated 1517, entitled "Das hoffgsindt Veneris" every character introduced himself in this manner:

> "Herr Donheuser bin ich genandt,
> Mein nam der ist gar weit erkandt,
> Aus Frankenlandt was ich geborn," etc.

As late as 1553 he used this type in "Der Eulenspiegel mit den blinden," where Eulenspiegel introduces himself as follows:

> "Eulenspiegel bin ich genandt," etc.

Expositional soliloquies of the narrative, descriptive, self-characterizing and intentional type occur on practically every page. Whenever the author feels that there is the least doubt about the story being absolutely clear to the audience, a character informs the spectators of his plans and intentions or tells them of some event that could not be presented on the stage. By means of soliloquies the author answers any possible questions as to the fate or experiences of a given character even before they arise.

The entire absence of scenery frequently makes the explanatory soliloquy necessary, so that the audience may know what the character is doing on the stage, and where he is located. So in "Fortunatus" the character states that he is now in a wild forest (Act 2) or in London (Act 5); in "Der hörnen Seifrit" the hero tells us that he is confronted by a high mountain (Act 3), etc. In "Der baur in dem fegfeur" the peasant gropes blindly about the stage and explains his actions by telling the audience that he is confined in a dark cell.

As all of the author's plays with the exception of a few shrovetide plays serve a moral purpose, as the epilogs of the comedies and tragedies and the concluding speeches of the shrovetide plays show, it is not surprising to find bits of moralizing in some of the soliloquies. One example taken from "Die schön Marina" will illustrate the type: "Unchastity is the most injurious of all vices. Whoever tries it is allured by it; whoever yields to it is choked by it; it weakens the understanding and shortens life, hurts one's reputation, consumes honor and wealth," etc. Other types of the thought soliloquy do not occur. Emotional soliloquies, however, especially those expressing the more common emotions such as grief, sorrow, rage, fear, regret, joy, etc., are met with very frequently.

It is interesting to note that Sachs gave some thought to the performance of his plays, as occasional stage directions will show. To be sure they are for the most part rather crude and one gesture is made to do service for differing emotions, reminding one forcibly of the acting of some of the present operatic stars. Soliloquies are usually without stage directions other than the stereotyped form: "enters and speaks," or "enters and speaks to him—or herself." But now and then the character is asked to clap the hands together above the head to express sorrow or grief or anger or what not. In Krimhilt's soliloquy at the end of "Seifrit" the author is liberal with stage directions: "She takes the twigs off of the corpse and beats her hands above her head"; then, a little later, "she sinks upon him, embraces and kisses him"; and later, "she sees the dagger, picks it up, looks at it, and says." At the end of the speech she leaves "sadly." The attempt to make the performance a little realistic certainly redounds to the credit of the author.

5. Herzog Heinrich Julius von Braunschweig

English drama, even in the crude form in which it was introduced to the Germans by the "Englische Komödianten," exerted a great influence upon German drama, especially upon Duke Heinrich's and Jakob Ayrer's plays. The Duke and Landgrave Maurice of Hessia each had a troop of English players and each was stimulated to the point of writing plays for these actors. Maurice, whose plays have been lost, even built a theater that was modeled after the type then in vogue in England. The Duke's plays show that he also adopted the English stage, whose chief characteristics were a balcony above the rear of the stage and the curtaining off of the space under the balcony, so that it could be employed when a change in the scene was desired.[1] More attention had been given to the art of acting in England than in Germany, and the plays of the English comedians are filled with elaborate stage-directions whose aim it was to secure great realism in presentation, especially when grief, pain and despair were to be depicted. All of the Duke's plays show his indebtedness in this respect, as they are abundantly supplied with stage-directions. English influence is also discernible in the use of prose, the introduction of instrumental music, songs and dances, and lastly in the adoption of the clown.

The soliloquies in the plays of the English comedians are very crude.[2] The characters often introduce themselves and speak at length about their plans and intentions. Sometimes these soliloquies are only indicated, e. g., in "Der König von Schottland," Act IV. The stage directions read: "The king comes out and tells how he is going to get to the place where Runcifax lives, whom he intends to ask which of his two daughters

---

[1] W. Creizenach, Die Schauspiele der englischen Komödianten, Vol. 23, D.N.L., p. 92.

[2] Ibid., p. 85.

he is to get." The villains expose their dark designs in soliloquy and the heroes announce both plans and accomplished facts, and sometimes give reports of actions that the audience has already witnessed. The moralizing soliloquy is frequently employed, but never at great length for fear of tiring the public. Ranting soliloquies in which passion was torn to tatters were also a favorite device.

What did the Duke adopt from this technic of the soliloquy? To secure realistic acting he supplied the soliloquies with full stage-directions in the manner of the English comedians. Then too he occasionally uses the ranting soliloquy, which in those days must have exerted a powerful influence upon the spectators. Good examples occur in the tragedy "Von einem ungerathenen Sohn," VI, end, where Nero is asked to accompany his ranting with such actions as: " grünselt, winselt, krümmet und windet sich, und stellet sich greulich an, brüllet wie ein Ochs, fället zu der Erden, kratzet mit Händen und Füssen von sich, stehet wieder auf und läuft herumb, als wenn er gar von Sinnen wäre."[1]   Another long speech of this type is found in the last act of " Buhler und Buhlerin," part of which reads: " Pfui dich, du stinkende Hoffart, pfui, du heillose und vergängliche Schminke! O wehe, o wehe, ach was leide ich Angst und Schmerz in meinem Herzen! O ihr Berge, fallet über mich und bedecket mich! Ach, dass die Erde sich aufthäte und mich verschlünge."[2]

For the most part the expositional soliloquies are crude, and often, as in the case of the clown, directly addressed to the audience. Sometimes a moralizing[3] or reflective bit and in one case a lyric prelude[4] raises the soliloquy to a slightly higher plane. The clown's soliloquies are either baldly expositional or reflective. In the latter he usually indulges in sardonic laughter[5] at the stupidity or the discomfiture of his master and frequently takes the audience into his confidence and begs them not to betray him.

---

[1] Julius Tittmann, Die Schauspiele des Herzog Heinrich Julius, Leipzig, 1880, p. 233.

[2] *Op. cit.*, p. 73.

[3] *Op. cit.*, p. 3. Susanna, p. 111–112, Von einem Edelmann.

[4] *Op. cit.*, pp. 35–6; Von einem Buhler.

[5] *Op. cit.*, pp. 64, 90, 96, 107, etc.

6. Jakob Ayrer

Two tendencies characterize Ayrer's work: an endeavor to remain faithful to the tradition of Sachs's dramatic art, together with an attempt to acclimate the histrionic art of the English comedians on the German stage. The result of this amalgamation produced no development in technic but rather a degeneration, as the plays show greater fondness for epic treatment than those of Sachs. To make up for the lack of interest resulting from this undramatic form he introduced elaborate stage processions, court scenes, battles and devil-scenes and reaches a higher plane in stage-effects, especially of the lurid melodramatic type. According to Robertson[1] the plays written between 1593 and 1598 show no English influence, whereas those between 1598 and 1605 reveal the influence of the English comedians. His stage probably consisted of a lower front stage and a raised stage or bridge, under the middle of which there was an opening which might be used for a cave or an additional place of entrance and exit or what not.[2] Rather full stage-directions, the use of the clown as a character in the plays, and instrumental music, all show English influence.

The expositional soliloquy is pressed into service on all possible occasions to acquaint the audience with the past, present and future, and little effort is made to raise them above the baldly instructive plane by giving them a reflective or emotional admixture. The moralizing element is usually confined to short sententious bits, although longer speeches do occur.[3] Emotional soliloquies are for the most part outbursts of grief and despair. These outbursts as a rule are rather tame affairs and seldom tear passion to tatters.[4] On the whole then Ayrer's soliloquies are a little cruder than those of Sachs.

[1] J. G. Robertson, Zur Kritik Jakob Ayres mit besonderer Rücksicht auf sein Verhältniss zu Hans Sachs und den englischen Komödianten, Leipzig, 1892.

[2] *Ibid.*

[3] Comedia von der schönen Sidea, II, beg. A. von Keller's ed.

[4] Keller, Vol. II, p. 787.

CHAPTER II

THE PSEUDO-CLASSIC DRAMA

1. *Gryphius*

There was a complete break with the old dramatic tradition in the 17th century when Andreas Gryphius, the originator of the German artistic drama, introduced the Renaissance tradition into German drama. Nothing in modern drama is based on medieval or 16th century drama. It really has its origin in the "Kunstdrama" of Gryphius, which is patterned after foreign models. The Silesian's model however was not so much Seneca as Vondel, the great Dutch dramatist, who was the leading exponent of the Renaissance tradition in Holland.

Seneca's style exerted an immeasurably greater influence upon Gryphius than his technic. "The technic of the two playwrights shows few points of contact,"[1] says Stachel. How do the two compare in the use of the soliloquy? Seneca, with one or two exceptions, invariably begins with an expositional soliloquy which is followed by a commenting chorus. Gryphius begins two of his five tragedies with a dialog, viz., "Leo Armenius" and "Cardenio und Celinde." In the second tragedy "Catherine von Georgien," after a prolog by Eternity in the style of the Church play prologs, the dialog form is employed. In "Carolus Stuardus" and "Papinianus" there are introductory expositional soliloquies but neither is followed by a chorus. In Seneca's plays the soliloquy forms a large component part, especially in "Medea," which has more soliloquy than dialog. The Roman poet shows a decided fondness for identifying soliloquies, a character often introducing himself to the audience before he begins a conversation. Another striking characteristic of his soliloquies is their position at the beginning of an act.

[1] Paul Stachel, Seneca und das deutsche Renaissance-Drama, Berlin, 1907, p. 270.

34

In Gryphius the soliloquy does not play so prominent a rôle. Although the length of the soliloquies leaves nothing to be desired, they are not so frequent, there are none of the identifying type, and there is no particular fondness shown for the beginning of an act.

Gryphius was endowed with a most melancholy temperament and the misfortunes that befell him and his country served to heighten this innate gloom. His five tragedies are permeated with pessimism as a result of his despairing outlook upon life. "All is vanity," or "sic transit gloria mundi" is in brief the theme of his plays. His heroes are characterized by steadfastness in enduring adversity rather than by positive action. The bombast and ranting, so characteristic of the plays, as well as the author's dejection and pessimism are faithfully mirrored in the soliloquies.

The initial expositional soliloquy in "Carolus Stuardus" is far from being baldly instructive. Several apostrophes, questions and answers, and an admixture of anger and defiance skillfully place the expositional matter into the background. The author's sermonizing instinct unfortunately got the better of him, and the fine frenzy of the closet dramatist is revealed in the line: "Bebt, die ihr herrscht und schafft! bebt ob dem Trauerspiel!" Once more, later in the play, the stage-illusion is destroyed when he has Fairfax say in a soliloquy: "Wer nah diss Unheil sieht, wer fern diss traurspiel hört." In "Papinianus" the expositional matter is also cleverly cloaked in the initial soliloquy. There is a considerable admixture of philosophical reflection:

> "Wer über alle steigt und von der stoltzen höh
> Der reichen ehre schaut, wie schlecht der pövel geh,
> . . . Hat wol (ich geb es nach) viel über die gemein.
> Ach! aber ach! wie leicht nimmt ihn der schwindel ein
> Und blendet unverhofft sein zitterndes gesichte,
> Dass er durch gähen fall wird, ehr man denkt, zu nichte!
> Wie leichte bricht der fels, auf dem er stand gefasst,
> Und reisst ihn mit sich ab!"

Later:

> " Wer die gemeine noth
> Zu lindern sich bemüht, sucht nichts als eignen tod.
> Wer sich für alle wagt, wird auch nicht einen finden,
> Auff dessen rechte treu er könn in schiffbruch gründen."

The speech is a real talking to one's self, apostrophe is freely used and in parts the dialog form is successfully employed:

> " Was hab ich denn verwürckt, unredliche gemütter?
> Kommt kläger! tretet vor! entdeckt, wie herb und bitter
> Auch eure zunge sey! Ich fliehe die gemein
> (Sprecht ihr) und schliesse mich vor freund und fremden ein.
> Wahr ists, dass ich," etc.

He takes up the charges one by one and answers them as though his accusers were confronting him.

There are few expositional soliloquies in the plays and all have an emotional coating. " Papinianus," V, furnishes a good example of inner conflict, the first time that we meet with this type of soliloquy. It opens with a question of perplexity: "What now?" then takes up the pros and cons, and after a short deliberation the decision is made:

> " Ach müssen wir die faust in seinem blute färben?
> Wir müssen! ach! es sey! Papinian soll sterben."

Another new type is found in " Catherine von Georgien " where Abas in a long soliloquy defends the decision he has made.

Ranting soliloquies in Gryphius are practically synonymous with emotional soliloquies, as he knows no bounds in the depiction of an emotion and regularly tears passion into tatters. In " Catherine " Abas pours forth pages such as the following:

> " Princessin! Ach! Princessin! Ach wir brennen!
> Feuer! Feuer! Feuer! Feuer! Feuer! kracht in diesem hertzen!
> Wir verlodern, wir verschmeltzen, angesteckt durch schwefel-
> kertzen
> Princessin! schau! princessin! wir bekennen
> Entzeptert, auf dem kny und mit gewundnen händen,
> Dass wir unrechtmässig dich betrübet,
> Dass wir ein stück an dir verübet,
> Welches aller zeiten zeit wird grausam nennen."

In "Leo Armenius":

"Treuloser aberwitz! durch wahn verführter mann!
Undank, dem laster selbst kein laster gleichen kann!
Durchteuffeltes gemüth! vermaledeyte sinnen!
Die keine redlichkeit noch wohlthat mag gewinnen!
Hab ich dich tollen hund vom koth in hof gebracht
Und auf selbst-eigner schoss berühmt und gross gemacht?
Hat uns die kalte schlang, die jetzund sticht, betrogen?
Ist dieser basilisc an unsrer brust erzogen?
Warum hat man dich nicht erwürgt auf frischer that?"

The exposition in "Cardenio und Celinde," though apparently in dialog form, is in reality one long soliloquy which is occasionally interrupted by a patient friend who asks for information that he is familiar with. In the same play, in the soliloquy at the beginning of the second act, we find a most interesting defense of the soliloquy, the first and only justification of this convention in German dramatic poetry:

"Was red ich? und mit wem? Wie, wenn die heisse macht
Der seuchen uns besiegt, ein zagend hertze schmacht
In hart entbrandter glut und die geschwächten sinnen
Empfinden nach und nach, wie kraft und geist zerinnen,
Indem die innre flamm nunmehr den sitz anfällt,
In welchem sich vernunfft gleich als beschlossen hält,
Denn taumelt der verstand, denn irren die gedanken,
Denn zehlt die schwartze zung des abgelebten krancken
Viel ungestalte wort in schwerem schwermen her."

In short, when disease or an all-consuming passion weaken body and mind, the mind is clouded and the ideas become confused and the tongue of the unfortunate victim rambles incoherently. Gryphius accordingly believes that a person soliloquizes only when he is in an abnormal condition.

According to Proelss these plays were produced on the stage, not very frequently to be sure and most likely in a sadly mutilated form. The stage varied according to the theater, the stages in the court and school theaters naturally being better equipped with stage setting and scenery than those of the traveling players. We still find a front and a back stage separated by a curtain, but the sides of the stage are now shut off from the audience either by curtains or walls. The front stage in the permanent theaters was provided with several drop curtains, one for each act; the stages of the itinerant players, on the other hand, generally had only one. Artificial light had to be used, as most of the performances were given indoors.

As we turn from the tragedies to the comedies—Scherzspiele is the author's designation—we involuntarily smile at the idea of an individual so immersed in gloom and melancholy even harboring a humorous thought. But as we read along we can but marvel at the wonderful metamorphosis, and finally perforce resort to a Dr. Jekyll and Mr. Hyde theory to account for the exuberant humor and the genuine tomfoolery that pervades the plays.

The expositional soliloquies are addressed directly to the audience and filled with such exclamations as: "See here! you may believe me," etc. Quite regularly the approach of the next character is announced at the end of a soliloquy: O see, there she comes already! or, See, there he is, etc. In "Die geliebte Dornrose" the overheard soliloquy is repeatedly used and in connection with it the aside. In the first act of this play two soliloquies, delivered by characters at opposite sides of the stage, are overheard by a third character who is hiding.[1] The asides are for the most part humorous, although a reflective bit occurs occasionally, so, e. g., "You see, neighbors, that's what you get when you allow the girls to go to school and learn to spell,"[2] possibly the earliest dramatic attack upon feminism.

Ranting soliloquies do not occur. A good example of the soliloquy expressing inner conflict occurs in "Horribilicribrifax": "What shall I do now? Shall I turn back? That would appear too unmannerly. I shall pass by and address her very briefly."[3] In "Peter Squenz," where there is a play within the play, viz., that of Pyramus and Thisbe, the characters of the enclosed play employ the introduction soliloquy in the style of the old church plays.[4]

---

[1] Comedies, ed. by H. Palm; I, p. 258 ff.; II, p. 286 ff.
[2] Ibid., p. 288.
[3] Ibid., II, p. 89. Another example in IV, p. 126.
[4] Ibid., III, p. 28 ff.

2. *Lohenstein*

Taking "Cleopatra" and "Ibrahim Sultan" as representative plays, one finds little in the use of the soliloquy that differentiates it from that employed by Gryphius. The relative scarcity of the soliloquy is perhaps noteworthy. The same fondness for philosophic reflections, florid rhetoric and apostrophe characterize Lohenstein's soliloquies. On the whole, there is less ranting than in the soliloquies of Gryphius. Quotations from the one real soliloquy in "Cleopatra"—there are three which are delivered in the presence of others—will sufficiently illustrate the above mentioned characteristics:

"O Sprudel-reiches Meer der jammer-vollen Welt!
Die Segel stehn gespann't, die Netze sind gestellt
Uns in den Hafen, Ihn in's Garn und Grab zu führen. . . .
Ein flatternd Herze gleicht mit Wanckel-muth den Pferden,
Die ein geschwancker Zaum bald recht- bald linckwerts lenckt. . . .
Gunst, Liebe, Freundschafft gleicht sich zarten Berg-Kristallen,
Die keine Kunst ergäntzt, sind einmal sie zerfallen:
Stillt auch Versöhnung gleich zuweilen Wund und Blutt,
Sie bricht erhitzter auf und schärffet Gall' und Glutt,
Die in dem Hertzen kocht, Man trockne Sumpf und Lachen,
Ein linder Regen wird sie wieder wässricht machen." . . .[1]

3. *Christian Weise*

Compared to the bombast and turgidity of Gryphius and his followers the simplicity and naturalness of Weise's plays is indeed refreshing. He shows a keen knowledge of human nature and a good sense of humor. Had he not ground out his plays in such a mechanical fashion—he wrote three each year besides attending to his arduous school work—and written them for school purposes, his plays might have exerted great influence upon the development of the drama. As a matter of fact his plays hardly created a ripple in the dramatic pool.

The comedies "Die böse Catherine" and "Der bäurische Machiavellus"[2] and the tragedy "Masaniello"[3] will adequately

[1] Act II, p. 181; Deutsche Nat. Lit., Vol. 36.
[2] Deutsche Nat. Lit., Vol. 39.
[3] Neudrucke deutscher Litteraturwerke des 16. und 17. Jahrhunderts, ed. by R. Petsch, Halle, 1907.

serve to illustrate Weise's use of the soliloquy. The large number of soliloquies is noteworthy as well as the author's fondness for asides. For the most part these soliloquies are expositional and of the crude type in which the audience is taken into the speaker's confidence. As a rule they are short and the language is natural and free from ornamentation. Our old friends, the self-identifying and self-characterizing soliloquy, also crop to the surface every now and then, so, e. g., in " Machiavellus," II and III ;[1] " Masaniello," III.[2] Reflective and moralizing soliloquies are rather infrequent, but it is interesting to notice that the clown is often the author's mouthpiece and indulges in a moralizing harangue in the style of the French raisonneur.[3] Emotional soliloquies are very prosaic and shallow and offer nothing remarkable.

On the whole, Weise's technic of the soliloquy shows little advance over that of the 15th and 16th centuries.

4. *Gottsched and his Followers*

Gottsched's view regarding the soliloquy has been previously quoted, viz., that sane people are not in the habit of talking to themselves when alone except when they are overcome by emotion, and in that case very briefly. Although he himself did not entirely taboo the soliloquy in his dramatic work—his " Cato," e. g., contains several short reflective and link soliloquies and a long deliberative soliloquy—his pupils and followers consistently avoided it. His " Deutsche Schaubühne," a collection of translations from Molière, Corneille, Racine, Voltaire, Holberg, etc., and original works by his wife, J. E. Schlegel and others, for the most part contains dramas which do without soliloquies and asides, especially the plays of J. E. Schlegel and Luise Adelgunde Victoria Gottsched, the reformer's wife. Schlegel makes sport of the soliloquy in a criticism of a drama by J. Klaj entitled " Herodes": " Here we plainly see how useful it would be if the author of the tragedy himself would step into a corner of the stage and talk occasionally.

---

1 Deutsche Nat. Lit., Vol. 39, p. 20; p. 45.
2 *Op. cit.*, p. 78.
3 *Ibid.*, p. 48.

. . . Instead of the hero coming out and telling himself about his troubles in a long speech, so that the spectators may know what is on his mind, the author might say: now love is tormenting my hero with cruel thoughts; now he does not know what to do."[1]

In the comedies the use of the confidant in the French manner solves the problem of exposition; in the tragedies the dialog is overloaded with epic matter, so that it becomes entirely undramatic and lifeless, as in Schlegel's " Hermann." Characterization and psychological development are practically wanting, in fact the whole treatment is epic rather than dramatic. If these plays had had real dramatic worth their new technic, viz., the dropping of soliloquies and asides, might have exerted great influence upon succeeding dramatists. As a matter of fact the innovation passed unnoticed.

Gottsched's hostility to the soliloquy and aside is doubtless due to French influence, primarily that of Hédelin, whom he ranks with Aristotle as an authority on dramatic matters.[2] Inasmuch as Hédelin's view was on the whole hostile to the soliloquy, as we have previously pointed out, it is small wonder that Gottsched adopts his master's point of view. Then too the fact that Corneille's later dramas and Molière's masterpieces were practically devoid of soliloquies may also have influenced him.

Summing up, then, the period from Gryphius to Lessing, a period of servile adherence to foreign models and foreign technic, Roman in the case of Gryphius, his followers and the writers of school drama, French in the case of Gottsched and his school, illustrates the usual fate of a popular idol in the career of the soliloquy. The florid, rhetorical soliloquy of Gryphius, dazzling the populace as did Beau Brummel in the heyday of his career, meets with reverses and is compelled to slink off the scene of its former triumphs, when it is reduced to a threadbare, impossible exterior such as it presents in Weise's works.

[1] Quoted by Düsel, in Beiträge zur Critischen Historie der deutschen Sprache, 27. Stück, 1741.
[2] F. Düsel, p. 4 ff.

CHAPTER III

THE ERA OF LESSING, SCHILLER AND GOETHE

In the preceding period the soliloquy passed from a state of unchallenged acceptance and unqualified approval to a state of innocuous desuetude. During the classic period, the era of Lessing, Schiller and Goethe, the soliloquy practically underwent the opposite process. Lessing attempted the impossible by trying to transmute a convention into a " slice of life." His realistic treatment of the soliloquy undoubtedly invested it with as much naturalness (vraisemblance, to use the French term), as was humanly possible, and yet the fact remains that even his form of the soliloquy is not a faithful counterpart of real life —we do not regularly think aloud—and after all a convention. Schiller and Goethe on the other hand did not worry about the naturalness or unnaturalness of the soliloquy, but restored it to its former position of an absolute ruler whose rights are in no wise questioned.

1. *Lessing*

If Lessing had not been antagonistic to all things Gottschedian, there is a possibility that he might have developed and perfected the new technic and given us powerful dramas whose appeal would not have been weakened by the absence of soliloquies and asides. But to return to actuality, Lessing's technic of the soliloquy in his early comedies, " Damon," " Der junge Gelehrte," " Der Misogyn," " Die alte Jungfer," " Der Freigeist," " Die Juden " and " Der Schatz," is on a plane so much lower than that found in his maturer plays that it is best treated separately.

Expositional soliloquies are rare in the early plays, as the employment of confidants in the French manner made them unnecessary. Only one example of the introductory expositional soliloquy occurs, viz., in " Der Misogyn," but even here

we find quite an improvement over the bald and calm statement of facts that was customary. A highly irate father bel-
lows a few disjointed expositional bits at the audience. A belated piece of introductory exposition, "Freigeist," I, 2, shows
a skillful blending of the purely epic with the emotional, the
latter outweighing the former. The accumulated anger of the
first scene bursts forth in wrathy reflections which are followed
by a few facts necessary to the comprehension of the plot. But
one crudely expositional speech can be found, that of Raps in
"Der Schatz," Sc. II, in which he identifies himself: "Man
muss allerlei Personen spielen können. Den möchte ich doch
sehen, der in diesem Aufzuge den Trommelschläger Raps
erkennen sollte? Ich seh' aus, ich weiss selber nicht wie; und
soll—ich weiss selber nicht was? Eine närrische Kommis-
sion!"

Unnecessary characterizing bits, which remind one of the
labels in the mouths of old pictures, crop up in soliloquies now
and then, e. g., in "Der Freigeist," I, end, where the servant
characterizes his master, and II, 4, where Lisette describes two
servants: "Ein Paar allerliebste Schlingel! Adrasts Johann
und Theophans Martin: die wahren Bilder ihrer Herren von
der hässlichen Seite! Aus Freigeisterei ist jener ein Spitzbube; und aus Frömmigkeit dieser ein Dummkopf."

The speaker's intention rarely requires a whole speech; as
a rule it forms the appendix of a reflective soliloquy, thus
giving a dramatic touch to speeches that temporarily retard the
movement of a play.[1]

Lessing shows a decided predilection for reflective soliloquies in the early plays, a type of soliloquy in which the speaker
reverts to the theme discussed in the preceding dialog and comments upon it or gives vent to the feeling and emotion aroused
by that conversation. Unless these reflective speeches result
in a change of attitude on the part of the speaker or in the
formulation of a plan that has some bearing on the action, they
naturally are lyric rather than dramatic. Most of them are
undramatic in character and have a considerable admixture of

[1] Die alte Jungfer, II, 4; Der Freigeist, III, 7; Der Schatz, Sc. 2.

philosophic reflection. "The tone of these soliloquies is naturally not dramatic but rather elegiac and passive, and philosophic embellishment which the young thinker could not do without even in his comedies makes them rather duller and more tiresome than livelier and brighter."[1] Every one of the early plays furnishes examples of this type: "Damon," Sc. 6, 8; "Der junge Gelehrte," I, I, II, 4; "Der Misogyn," II, beg. II, 6; II, end; "Die alte Jungfer," II, 4; "Die Juden," 17, 19; "Der Schatz," 3, 8, 10, 11; "Der Freigeist," III, 3, III, 7, V, 2, etc. There is a liberal sprinkling of the philosophical element in almost all of the above mentioned soliloquies. A full-fledged "Tendenzmonolog" occurs in "Die Juden," Sc. 3, in which the attitude of Christians towards Jews is criticized. Emotional outbursts are rare, the best examples occurring in "Der Freigeist," I, 2, V, 2.

Lessing's desire to avoid an empty stage gave rise to quite a few link soliloquies whose function it was to fill the gap between the exit of one character and the entrance of another.[2]

The most interesting feature of Lessing's early soliloquies is their style. Even in "Damon," his earliest attempt, Lessing breaks away from the familiar type with its carefully expressed, logically developed and uninterrupted ideas, such as one might find and expect in a previously prepared argument or oration. Both of Damon's long reflective speeches, Sc. 6 and 8, show the author's attempt to express the ideas as they occur to the speaker. The thoughts come haltingly one moment, then again one thought is interrupted by another that suddenly suggests itself. There are breaks in the continuity of the thought, sudden jumps far afield, reversion to previously expressed ideas, sudden anticipations. "Ich würde ihn selbst tadeln—Doch—ich halte ihn auch nicht einmal fähig dazu—er mag sein, was er will—aber—ich irre mich wohl auch—ich beurtheile ihn nach mir—weil ich so schwach bin; folgt es denn daraus, dass ein anderer—Doch allerdings eine so vollkommene Freundschaft ist für diese Welt nicht—Ob auch wohl Leander so denkt, als er redet?—Halt—Ich will," etc.

1 Düsel, *op. cit.*, p. 30.
2 Damon, I, 3; I, 5; Die alte Jungfer, 1, 3; I, 4; Der junge Gelehrte, I, 1.

In his desire to emphasize the realistic element he over-emphasized and went too far, but that does not detract from the value of the innovation. There is at least no doubt in any one's mind that the speaker is thoroughly aroused and excited. Adrast's soliloquy in " Der Freigeist," V, 2, also admirably portrays his violent agitation: "Was für ein neuer Streich!—Ich kann nicht wieder zu mir kommen!—Es ist nicht auszuhalten! Verachtungen, Beleidigungen—Beleidigungen in dem Gegenstande, der ihm der liebste sein muss:—alles ist umsonst; nichts will er fühlen," etc.

The occasional interruption of the speaker in the middle of his soliloquy is another realistic touch.[1] But the announcing of the next character by the speaker of the soliloquy when he has finished is far more common: "Da kömmt er ja selber; Ah, hui da kömmt; Ha, da kömmt er; kömmt da nicht."

Apostrophe is rarely used in the early plays to enliven the soliloquy. A long apostrophe to learning by Damis occurs in a pseudo-soliloquy, as a servant is present and listening.[2]

Asides are numerous, especially in " Die Juden," " Der Freigeist," and " Der Schatz." It seems strange that the same man who strove to make the soliloquy realistic could allow such an improbable convention as the aside in his plays. During a dialog in " Die Juden," e. g., the characters stop in the middle of a conversation and each delivers three asides, a ludicrous performance. Then after they have talked past each other, one asks the other why he has been so lost in thought.[3] Of course Lessing's indebtedness to French comedy and especially to Regnard, Marivaux and Destouches accounts for the use of the aside, but as early as 1750, the same year in which " Der Schatz " was written, he found asides "so ungereimt, dass nichts darüber ist,"[4] and accused every one who did not find them very offensive of lack of taste. It is evidently another instance of the fact that theory and practise do not always coincide.

---

[1] Die alte Jungfer, II, 4; Der Freigeist, V, 2; Die Juden, I, 3; I, 19.
[2] Der Junge Gelehrte, I, 1.
[3] Sc. 6.
[4] Criticism of Plautus' Captivi in Beyträge zur Historie u. Aufnahme des Theaters, 3. Stück, 1750.

In the 48th number of the "Hamburgische Dramaturgie" Lessing warmly defends soliloquies which acquaint us with the attitude and the plans of the speaker. Quoting from his translation of Diderot's essay on dramatic art he says: "Warum haben gewisse Monologen eine so grosse Wirkung? Darum, weil sie mir die geheimen Anschläge einer Person vertrauen und diese Vertraulichkeit mich den Augenblick mit Furcht oder Hoffnung füllet." He goes on to say that if the attitude of the characters is unknown to the spectator the latter cannot manifest particular interest in the action, but that his interest will be doubled if he has some light on the matter and feels that the action and the speeches would be entirely different if the characters knew each other. Only in that case he will hardly be able to await the development when he is able to compare their real selves with their acts. Later in the same essay he defends the expositional prologs of Euripides because he maintains that it is better to acquaint the audience with the necessary exposition in a crude manner than not at all. In No. 49 he again champions the expositional prolog and states that he greatly prefers it to a dialog exposition with the aid of a talkative confidant.

Lessing practised what he preached with regard to the soliloquy, and we find expositional soliloquies of all kinds, including the introductory variety as well as soliloquies which reveal the thoughts and emotions of the speakers. Initial exposition is conveyed in soliloquy form in "Philotas" and "Emilia Galotti," in dialog form in "Miss Sara Sampson," "Minna," and "Nathan." In both "Minna" and "Sara" this expositional dialog takes place between the principal characters and a trusted servant or chambermaid, in other words the French confidant; in "Nathan" the dialog is better motivated, as Nathan returns from a journey and naturally wishes to be put in touch with the events that have occurred during his absence, reminding one somewhat of Ibsen's technic in "Ghosts," "Rosmersholm," "Doll's House" and others.

The brief expositional bit in "Minna" in which Just conveys a few facts while talking in his sleep is too short to be a full-fledged initial exposition soliloquy. The clever manner in which its exposition is presented, with its admixture of anger and the use of the dialog form, brings home rather forcibly the remarkable progress since the old-time expositional soliloquy. The initial soliloquy in " Philotas " is so permeated with despair, impatience, disgust and impotent rage that one fails to notice the purely expositional element. It is a real talking to one's self: " Schmeichle dir nur, Philotas! " and uses the apostrophe very effectively. Of the eight scenes in the first act of " Emilia Galotti," the odd scenes are adjoining links in the exposition, all in soliloquy form and all delivered by the prince. Only the first scene includes small bits of dialog with his valet. But this exposition is cleverly managed. In the first two letters in the mass of mail which he is rapidly perusing are pegs upon which he hangs a bit of information. Then the arrival of a painting previously ordered furnishes a very plausible excuse for a little more exposition. Scene 5 alone is a little superfluous in my opinion, inasmuch as the declaration of his love is repeated in the dialog of the following scene. To be sure the prince's agitation gives this soliloquy life and animation, but it is not essential. The seventh scene on the other hand bears vitally upon what is to follow with its anticipatory content. Incidentally this series of soliloquies throws considerable light upon the character of the prince.

Self-characterizing passages occur in several of the soliloquies, the crudest being that of the Klosterbruder in " Nathan," who says: " Ich mag nicht fein sein; mag nicht überreden; mag mein Näschen nicht in alles stecken; mag mein Händchen nicht in allem haben."[1] Marwood's speech, IV, 5, is more dramatic: " Bin ich allein?—Kann ich unbemerkt einmal Atem schöpfen und die Muskeln des Gesichtes in ihre natürliche Lage fahren lassen?—Ich muss geschwind einmal in allen Mienen die wahre Marwood sein, um den Zwang der Verstellung wieder aushalten zu können.—Wie hasse ich dich, niedrige Verstellung! Nicht weil ich die Aufrichtigkeit liebe sondern weil du die armseligste Zuflucht der ohnmächtigen Rachsucht bist."[2] When Tellheim tears up Marloff's note, he throws a

[1] Nathan der Weise, IV, beginning.
[2] Miss Sara Sampson.

little light on his character: "Wer steht mir dafür, dass eigner Mangel mich nicht einmal verleiten könnte, Gebrauch davon zu machen?"[1]

Baldly expositional bits are rare indeed, the two instances in "Minna" being the only examples. But even here they are partially redeemed by being but a part of respectable reflective soliloquies. A little thought, however, would have made them unnecessary.

A good example of a descriptive soliloquy occurs in "Emilia Galotti," III, 2, where Marinelli stands at the window and describes what is going on outside. Questions and exclamations together with apostrophes give it quite a little dramatic life. Other descriptive passages are found in "Nathan," II, 5, II, 7, in the first of which Nathan describes the approaching knight, in the second a former acquaintance.

When a speaker expresses his intention in soliloquy he usually does so after due reflection, and accordingly we find an intentional ending in practically all reflective soliloquies as well as in some of the deliberative and conflict soliloquies. In this respect the reflective soliloquies of the later plays stand on a higher plane, as they rise from passive inactivity to active participation in the plot.

The reflective soliloquies of the later plays, then, both revert and anticipate, thus influencing the action. A good example ocurs in "Nathan," IV, 8, where Daja, after reflecting for a moment about the preceding conversation, announces her intention of telling Recha who she really is. Other examples are found in "Minna," IV, 8; "Philotas," Sc. 4; "Emilia," III, 5, III, 2. The moralizing and philosophical element which Lessing was so partial to in his early plays is discarded in his later dramas.

The best example of a deliberative soliloquy is Nathan's famous speech, III, 6, in which he arrays his keen mental powers against the Sultan's tricky question that covers so many pitfalls and finally hits upon a solution. The slight perplexity that the Sultan's question has left him in is splendidly portrayed:

[1]Minna, I, 7.

"Hm! Hm!—wunderlich!—Wie ist
Mir denn?—Was will der Sultan? Was?—Ich bin
Auf Geld gefasst; und er will—Wahrheit. Wahrheit."

Then after he has laid bare the trap he proceeds to weigh possible answers in masterly fashion:

"Ich muss
Behutsam gehn.—und wie? wie das?—So ganz
Stockjude sein zu wollen, geht schon nicht.—
Und ganz und gar nicht Jude geht noch minder.
Denn, wenn kein Jude, dürft er nur fragen,
Warum kein Muselman?"

In the ensuing pause a solution presents itself which satisfies him completely: "Das war's. Das kann mich retten."

Scene 8 of the same act makes it plain that to Lessing the soliloquy was a thinking aloud. The stage directions read: "Tempelherr. Geht mit sich selbst kämpfend, auf und ab; bis er losbricht," which surely indicates that we are now to hear the continuation of an inner conflict, that his thoughts now become audible. His emotion quickly gives way to calmer deliberation, which results in a decision. This transition from silent to audible thought is also evident in V, 3, and III, 6.

When the head is subordinated to the heart, when the careful mental balancing of the pros and cons is upset by an emotional eruption, we pass from the deliberative soliloquy to one of conflict. Odoardo's speech, V, 4, aptly illustrates this transition: "Wie?—Nimmermehr!—Mir vorschreiben, wo sie hin soll?— Mir sie vorenthalten?—Wer will das? Wer darf das?—Der hier alles darf, was er will? Gut, gut; so soll er sehen, wie viel auch ich darf, ob ich es schon nicht dürfte! Kurzsichtiger Wüterich! Mit dir will ich es schon aufnehmen. Wer kein Gesetz achtet, ist eben so mächtig, als wer kein Gesetz hat. Das weisst du nicht? Komm an! komm an!—Aber siehe da! Schon wieder; schon wieder rennet der Zorn mit dem Verstande davon." Then he settles down to calm deliberation: "Was will ich? Erst müsst' es doch geschehen sein, worüber ich tobe," etc. Soliloquies in which emotion unmistakably holds the upper hand are Odoardo's conflict soliloquy, V, 6; Mellefont's speech, IV, 2; Marwood's soliloquy, IV, 9; the speech of

Tempelherr, III, 10. Philotas's long soliloquy in the 4th scene is deliberative on the whole, although there is a strong undercurrent of emotion at times.

Purely emotional soliloquies, i. e., soliloquies whose sole aim is to acquaint us with the speaker's feelings, are not frequent. Most of the soliloquies, with the exception of the baldly expositional and the purely mental deliberative speeches, have an admixture of emotion. Minna's outburst of joy at finding Tellheim: "Ich habe ihn wieder!—Ich hab' ihn, ich hab' ihn! Ich bin glücklich! und fröhlich!"[1] is the best example of an unadulterated emotional soliloquy in Lessing's dramas.

The language of the soliloquies in the later plays lacks poetic embellishment and rhetorical flourish; it is simple and natural. Liberal use of apostrophe and the dialog form infuses a great deal of dramatic life into these speeches. In addition the soliloquies give us an insight into the workings of the mind, showing us how the ideas come to consciousness one by one. The fact that the ego of the speaker is so often divided into two arguing or opposing selves makes us forget for the time being that there is but one character on the stage.

The custom of announcing the approach of an actor at the close of the soliloquy is retained in the later plays. Asides are less numerous in the later dramas, but even this is surprising when we know how bitterly Lessing denounced them in the "Dramaturgie," where he refers to them as "unnatürliche Künsteleien." "Nathan" contains as many as fifteen asides!

Nowhere in Lessing's plays is the language of the soliloquy embellished or florid. Generalizing and sententious ingredients occur only in his early plays. A growing desire to make the soliloquies as natural as possible is plainly discernible as one reads the dramas chronologically. Whereas many of the early soliloquies served a merely mechanical purpose, viz., the linking of scenes, the later soliloquies are essential parts of the drama as they have a direct bearing upon plot and characterization. The scarcity of expositional soliloquies in the early plays is due to the fact that the necessary exposition was usually

[1] II, 7.

conveyed to the audience by dialogs of servants or confidants who were thoroughly conversant with the state of affairs. Although the later plays have more expositional soliloquies, these speeches are never crudely instructive but closely knit into the fabric of the play.

2. *Storm and Stress Drama*

A craving for uncorrupted nature, the glorification of individuality, the denunciation of current social conditions, bitter attacks upon authority, whatever its guise—these in short are the characteristics of this revolutionary movement. The attack upon literary authority manifested itself chiefly in a revolt against French influence, French artificiality and the unnaturalness that resulted from the tyranny of the irksome three unities, together with a demand for themes that were distinctively German in character.

How did all this affect the technic of the soliloquy? Quantitatively there is little difference, with the exception of a few plays, notably Schiller's " Die Räuber," and Müller's "Genoveva," where restraint is thrown to the winds and the soliloquy is allowed to flood page after page. Qualitatively, however, the general tendency is to indulge in ranting and produce weird excrescences upon the tree of sane expression. But whatever their faults these soliloquies are for the most part highly dramatic and virile. They show many of the best traits of Lessing's technic with their use of the dialog form, of apostrophe, frequent pauses and the presentation of ideas as they occur to the speaker.

Schiller's and Goethe's storm and stress plays will be discussed in connection with their other dramas. The dramas to be considered here are Klinger's " Die Zwillinge," Leisewitz's " Julius von Tarentum," Wagner's " Die Kindermörderin," Lenz's "Der Hofmeister," and Müller's "Golo und Genoveva."[1]

Sauer's criticism: " Wie ein einziger Monolog braust das Stück dahin,"[2] is justified as Guelfo rages through " Die Zwillinge " like a Titan surrounded by pygmies. Although the solil-

[8] Stürmer und Dränger, 3 vols. ed. by A. Sauer, Berlin.
[2] *Ibid.*, Vol. 1, p. 311.

oquies are not as numerous as one might expect, many of Guelfo's speeches hardly bear the semblance of dialog and are in reality disguised soliloquies. So, in I, 2, Guelfo is interrupted by Grimaldi with "Lieber Guelfo, nicht so," after he has torn a goodly supply of passion to tatters, but he pays absolutely no attention to the remark. Eight of the nine soliloquies fall to the share of Guelfo and all are hot with rage and anger, with the exception of the first half of his soliloquy at the end of Act III. Exclamations, apostrophes, questions and pauses admirably portray his tempest-tossed soul. The following will illustrate the style: "Ha! verfolgt mich alles? Alle Dämonen und Gespenster der Nacht? Mein böser Geist hängt mir auf dem Nacken, er lässt mich nicht, stiert mich aus allen Winkeln an. Blas zu! Vergift mir jedes Fäserchen meines Herzens! Wühl giftig in meinem Blut! Hu! was martert den Guelfo? wen will Guelfo martern?—Die Glocke ruft dumpf, der Sturm saust über die Tiber. Eine schöne Nacht!—Ferdinando, gieb das Weib! Ferdinando gieb die Erstgeburt!"[1] The language throughout leaves the impression of a battlefield covered with the disjecta membra of the combatants.

Müller's "Golo und Genoveva" is top-heavy with soliloquies and asides. The soliloquies are often baldly narrative and descriptive, but together with these expositional speeches we find reflective soliloquies and a choice assortment of emotional outbursts, mostly by Golo, who supplies at least one example for every emotion aroused by unrequited love. The language every now and then is lost in a maze of florid ingredients, as, e. g., "Hier will ich die süsse Luft einschlürfen, die ihre schöne Wange gekühlt, darein sie ihren balsamischen Atem ergoss; begrabt mich hier, wenn ich einst sterbe, mein Leib wird nicht in Staub zerfallen, alle meine erstarrte Adern werden bald in ein neues Leben zurückdringen und wie Blumen durch die Erde zu dieser Luft emporschiessen.—Wer doch der Schlummer sein könnte, auf solch einem Paar Wimpern zu ruhen.— Kalter Tod, warmes Leben; alles um sie—die Welt, das Universum—um einem einzigen Druck."

[1] III, 1.

"Schlaf wohl und süss, Liebchen zart,
Auf deinem Mund meine Himmelfahrt!"[1]

The language of the soliloquies in the other plays mentioned before is natural and appropriate to the characters. In "Der Hofmeister" and "Die Kindermörderin" the few soliloquies are interesting because of the rather full stage-directions calling for pantomime, so, e. g.: "setzt sich hin und liest eine Zeit lang"; legt das Buch hin, geht sehr bewegt ein paarmal auf und ab"; "sucht in der Tasche und zieht den Brief heraus. Guckt ihn noch einmal durch."[2] Silence on the stage and silent expression of the emotions is an interesting forerunner of modern realistic methods. That soliloquies may have their uses is made clear by one of the characters in "Der Hofmeister" who begins to soliloquize in another's presence and, when interrupted, explains: "Es ist ein Monolog aus einem Trauerspiel, den ich gern recitiere wenn ich Sorgen habe,"[3] in other words, an efficacious means of driving dull care away. The soliloquy is often a real talking to one's self, as in "Julius von Tarentum," II, 7: "Dummkopf, sie sagte mir ja selbst die Ursach meiner Kälte"; V, 2, "Alter, ist das der Ton eines Richters?" In this play especially the soliloquies contain frequent pauses, numerous apostrophes and the dialog form.

3. Schiller

The most striking fact about the soliloquy in Schiller is its frequent occurrence in the early plays, especially "Die Räuber," and its gradual curtailment and disappearance in the latter plays. That Schiller gave this convention more than passing thought is evidenced in his preface[4] to the "Räuber," where he speaks with approval of the self-revealing soliloquy, the soliloquy which acquaints us with the inmost thoughts and feelings of the speaker. To be sure, he does not directly mention the soliloquy, but he does speak of "surprising the soul as it were in its most secret movements" (die Seele gleichsam bei ihren

[1] II, 4, end.
[2] IV, p. 325, Die Kindermörderin. V, beginning.
[3] II, 5.
[4] First sentence of the Vorrede.

geheimsten Operationen ertappen) as an advantage of the dramatic method and this undoubtedly refers to the convention of the soliloquy.

Quite in accordance with this statement we find a preponderance of reflective and emotional soliloquies and a comparative scarcity of the purely expositional type. In fact, most of the expositional soliloquies form a small component part of some other type of soliloquy. There is but an isolated example of an initial exposition soliloquy, and that does not occur in a play proper but in the prolog to the "Jungfrau von Orleans."[1] In it Joan acquaints us with the supernatural message which she has received.

Near the beginning of "Die Räuber" Franz prefaces a long reflective soliloquy with a bit of self-characterization that leaves no doubt as to his villainy, e. g., "Da müsst ich ein erbärmlicher Stümper sein, wenn ich's nicht einmal so weit gebracht hätte, einen Sohn vom Herzen des Vaters loszulösen. . . ."[2] Another example of this type occurs in "Maria Stuart," where Elizabeth throws considerable light upon her character: "O Sklaverei des Volksdiensts! Schmähliche Knechtschaft—Wie bin ich's müde, diesem Götzen zu schmeicheln, den mein Innerstes verachtet! etc."[3] Apostrophes, exclamations, questions and answers impart considerable life to these expositional fragments and raise them far above the old *ad spectatores* speeches.

Narrative soliloquies are scarce, and when they do occur they are incorporated in a reflective or emotional speech. In Wallenstein's reflective soliloquy, III, 13, we find quite a bit of narration:

> "Dahingeschmolzen vor
> Der schwed'schen Stärke waren eure Heere,
> Am Lech sank Tilly, euer letzter Hort;
> Ins Bayerland, wie ein geschwollner Strom,
> Ergoss sich dieser Gustav, und zu Wien
> In seiner Hofburg zitterte der Kaiser,
> Soldaten waren teuer, etc." [4]

[1] Scene 4 entire.
[2] I, 1.
[3] IV, 10.
[4] Wallensteins Tod.

Beatrice, in her first long emotional soliloquy, also contributes expositional material in the form of narration beginning:

> "Und so erwuchs ich still am stillen Orte,
> In Lebensglut den Schatten beigesellt,
> Da stand er plötzlich an des Klosters Pforte,
> Schön wie ein Gott, und männlich wie ein Held."[1]

Wallenstein's narrative is infused with dramatic life by the use of the apostrophe, that of Beatrice by exclamation.

A splendid example of dramatic description is found in Leicester's soliloquy, V, 10,[2] in which the preparations for the execution and the execution itself are vividly sketched:

> "... Horch! Was war das?
> Sie sind schon unten ... Unter meinen Füssen
> Bereitet sich das fürchterliche Werk.
> Ich höre Stimmen—Fort! Hinweg! Hinweg
> Aus diesem Haus des Schreckens und des Todes!
> Wie? Fesselt mich ein Gott an diesen Boden?
> Muss ich anhören, was mir anzuschauen graut?
> Die Stimme des Dechanten—Er ermahnet sie—
> Sie unterbricht ihn—Horch!—Laut betet sie—
> Mit fester Stimme—Es wird still—Ganz still!
> Nur schluchzen hör' ich und die Weiber weinen—
> Sie wird entkleidet—Horch! Der Schemel wird
> Gerückt—Sie kniet aufs Kissen—legt das Haupt—"

Other examples worthy of mention are "Maria Stuart," IV, 10, where Elizabeth depicts the dangers that threaten her on every side; "Die Jungfrau von Orleans," IV, beginning, where Joan describes the festivities in Rheims; II, 6, of the same play, where Montgomery describes the approach of the battling maiden.

The speaker's intention usually forms the conclusion of a reflective or deliberative soliloquy and is short as a rule: "Fiesco," II, 8, II, 19, III, 2, V, 1; "Maria Stuart," IV, 10; "Jungfrau," III, 9; "Kabale und Liebe," I, 7; "Wallensteins Tod," III, 13. When Franz Moor learns of his father's death he indulges in a lengthy instructive outburst which illustrates

---

[1] Die Braut von Messina.
[2] Maria Stuart.

the ranting unnatural style so characteristic of "Die Räuber":
"Nun sollt ihr den nackten Franz sehen und euch entsetzen!
Meine Augenbrauen sollen über euch herhangen wie Gewitter-
wolken, mein herrischer Name schweben wie ein drohender
Komet über diesen Gebirgen, meine Stirne soll euer Wetterglas
sein! Er streichelte und koste den Nacken, der gegen ihn
störrig zurückschlug. Streicheln und kosen ist meine Sache
nicht. Ich will euch die zackichten Sporen ins Fleisch hauen,
und die scharfe Geissel versuchen. . . . In meinem Gebiet
soll's so weit kommen, dass Kartoffeln und dünn Bier ein
Traktament für Festtage werden, und wehe dem, der mir mit
vollen, feurigen Backen unter die Augen tritt! Blässe der
Armut und sklavischen Furcht sind meine Leibfarbe; in diese
Liverei will ich euch kleiden!"[1]
Thought soliloquies, especially of the reflective variety,
greatly outnumber the expositional type, and every play furnishes one or more examples. In "Die Räuber" Franz is
especially obliging in the matter of taking the audience into his
confidence and unfolding his crassly materialistic point of view,
his heartless villainy, his cringing cowardice. In his first long-
winded soliloquy he reveals his attitude toward life, practically
a negation of all ties which hold society together. One by one
he takes up and coolly disposes of reputation, conscience, etc.:
"Gewissen—o ja freilich! ein tüchtiger Lumpenmann, Sper-
linge von Kirschbäumen wegzuschrecken! . . . In der That
sehr lobenswürdige Anstalten die Narren im Respekt und den
Pöbel unter dem Pantoffel zu halten, damit die Gescheiten es
desto bequemer haben."[2] In spite of its great length the soliloquy
is not without dramatic life. Apostrophes are frequent, questions follow each other in breathless haste, sometimes five or
six before an answer is vouchsafed: "Warum hat er mich
gemacht? doch wohl nicht gar aus Liebe zu mir, der erst ein
Ich werden sollte? Hat er mich gekannt ehe er mich machte?
Oder hat er mich gedacht wie er mich machte? Oder hat er
mich gewünscht, da er mich machte? Wusste er was ich
werden würde? Das wollte ich ihm nicht raten."[2] Occa-

[1] Die Räuber, II, 2 end.
[2] I, 1.

sional interruptions in the flow of thought also show a desire to secure verisimilitude. In the same act Karl reflects upon the degeneracy of the times in a speech that is permeated with disgust and indignation and characterized by terrible ranting.[1] The soliloquy at the beginning of the second act, partly reflective, partly deliberative, suffers from the insertion of medical lore in the reflective portion, but is otherwise dramatic. The other reflective speeches in this play are made more or less dramatic by the use of exclamations, questions and answers, and pauses.[2]

The short reflective soliloquies in " Fiesco " form quite a contrast to the lengthy outpourings in " Die Räuber." Their brevity might tempt one to regard them as link soliloquies, but they serve a dramatic purpose by characterizing the speaker or by showing his attitude. Fiesco delivers most of these speeches, usually at the end of a scene: " Dieser Republikaner ist hart wie Stahl." " Wenn diese Flammen ins Vaterland schlagen, mögen die Doria feste stehen." Other instances occur in I, 2; II, 16; III, 6; V, 1.

It would lead too far afield to take up all the reflective soliloquies. Among the more noteworthy[3] are Eboli's dramatic speech when Don Karlos spurns her love,[4] Wallenstein's long soliloquy when he realizes that he has hopelessly involved himself,[5] Leicester's speech after his unmasking by Burleigh,[6] Tell's famous soliloquy in the hollow way.[7] The length of Tell's speech is a little surprising at first sight, but, let us remember that we are dealing with a soliloquy, not with dialog. In dialog his loquaciousness would be surprising, but here it is simply a case of his thoughts being made audible as he is waiting to kill Gessler. This reflective speech contains no element of conflict; no at-

[1] I, 2.
[2] I, end; IV, 2 by Franz; IV, 2, end by Franz; IV, 4.
[3] Other examples: Kabale und Liebe, I, 6; IV, 8; Don Karlos, I, 1; II, 9; III, 1; III, 5; IV, 6. Piccolomini, II, 5; III, 9; Wallensteins Tod, II, 4; II, 5; III, 13. Jungfrau, II, 8; III, 9; Braut v. Messina, beg. of Sc. 2 partly; Tell, II, 1 end.
[4] Don Karlos, II, 9.
[5] Wallensteins Tod, I, 4.
[6] Maria Stuart, IV, 4.
[7] Wilhelm Tell, IV, 3.

tempt is made to reach a decision, no defense of his intended action is made. His decision is previously made and he is absolutely convinced of the righteousness of his undertaking. The form is practically that of a dialog and consequently highly dramatic. Practically a third of it is an apostrophe to Gessler, and throughout the remainder of the soliloquy apostrophes are made now to his arrow and bowstring, now to his children.

Purely deliberative soliloquies are rather infrequent, inasmuch as the speaker's emotional nature usually crops to the surface and puts an end to calm deliberation and a cool unimpassioned weighing of the pros and cons. Franz Moor's solution of the problem of committing murder legally admirably illustrates the deliberative type. The problem is stated: "Wer es verstünde dem Tod diesen ungebahnten Weg in das Schloss des Lebens zu ebnen? den Körper vom Geist aus zu verderben . . . ha! ein Originalwerk! wer das zu Stand brächte?" His perplexity is removed little by little by a careful weighing of all possible solutions, till the one eminently satisfactory weapon is found: "Zorn? . . . dieser heisshungrige Wolf frisst sich zu schnell satt . . . Sorge? . . . dieser Wurm nagt mir zu langsam . . . Gram? . . . diese Natter schleicht mir zu träge—Furcht? . . . die Hoffnung lässt sie nicht umgreifen . . . Was? sind das all die Henker des Menschen? . . . Ist das Arsenal des Todes so bald erschöpft? . . . (Tiefsinnend) Wie? . . . Nun? . . . Was? Nein! Ha! (Auffahrend) Schreck!—Was kann der Schreck nicht? . . . Und doch? Wenn er auch diesem Sturm stünde? . . . Wenn er? etc."[1] The final decision is worked out as well as any of Lessing's. The suspense, the mental groping, the flashlike decision, remind us of Nathan's decision in his famous soliloquy. To be sure the ranting spoils the good effect. Posa's soliloquy immediately before his interview with the king is moulded along the lines of Nathan's speech prior to his interview with the Sultan and avoids Moor's ranting. Posa is perplexed at being summoned by the king. "Wie komm ich aber hieher? Eigensinn des launenhaften Zufalls war es nur, was mir mein Bild in diesen Spiegeln zeigte? . . .

[1] Die Räuber, II, 1.

Ein Zufall nur?" After due deliberation he reaches a decision: "Was der König mit mir auch wollen mag, gleichviel!—Ich weiss, was ich . . . ich mit dem König soll—und wär's auch eine Feuerflocke Wahrheit nur. . . ."[1] The Moor's soliloquy in Fiesco[2] differs from these in that it reaches no decision.

When the speaker's emotions intrude upon his calm deliberation, when head gives way to the heart, the way is paved for a soliloquy in which the struggle between conflicting ideas and emotions is depicted, in short, a conflict soliloquy. Fiesco passes through two such struggles. In the first conflict[3] between his selfishness and his altruism the latter is victorious and he decides to renounce his ambition for the good of the state. The opening lines leave no doubt as to the type of soliloquy: "Welch ein Aufruhr in meiner Brust! welche heimliche Flucht der Gedanken. . . ." In his second inner struggle[4] Fiesco vacillates for some time between obeying and ruling, but finally decides in favor of the hammer rather than the anvil. Here too the inner unrest is pointed out near the opening of the soliloquy: "Wilde Phantasien haben meinen Schlaf aufgeschwelgt . . . mein ganzes Wesen krampfig um eine Empfindung gewälzt. . . ." Joan's conflict between love and duty,[5] Karl Moor's "to be or not to be" soliloquy,[6] Amalia's struggle after she has spoken to Karl,[7] and the latter's conflict as he sees the scenes of his childhood after a long absence,[8] are other examples of this type.[9]

Philosophic utterances frequently form a small component part of a reflective soliloquy, especially in the later dramas. The most noteworthy example, as well as the longest, is Wallenstein's reflection on custom:[10]

---

[1] Don Karlos, III, 9.
[2] Fiesco, III, 7.
[3] Die Verschwörung des Fiesco, II, 19.
[4] Fiesco, III, 2.
[5] Die Jungfrau, v. O, IV, beg.
[6] Die Räuber, IV, 5.
[7] *Ibid.*, IV, 4.
[8] *Ibid.*, IV. 1.
[9] Two soliloquies in Demetrius.
[10] Wallensteins Tod, I, 4.

"Nicht was lebendig, kraftvoll sich verkündigt,
Ist das gefährlich Furchtbare. Das ganz
Gemeine ist's, das ewig Gestrige,
Was immer war und immer wiederkehret
Und morgen gilt, weil's heute hat gegolten!
Denn aus Gemeinem ist der Mensch gemacht,
Und die Gewohnheit nennt er seine Amme.
Weh dem, der an den würdig alten Hausrat
Ihm rührt, das teure Erbstück seiner Ahnen!"

In the face of death Talbot philosophizes as follows:

"So geht der Mensch zu Ende—und die einzige
Ausbeute, die wir aus dem Kampf des Lebens
Wegtragen ist die Einsicht in das Nichts
Und herzliche Verachtung alles dessen,
Was uns erhaben schien und wünschenswert. . . ."[1]

Other examples occur in "Don Karlos," III, 9; "Maria Stuart," II, 6; IV, 10; "Wilhelm Tell," II, 1.

Emotional soliloquies are especially numerous in "Die Räuber," and the early dramas are all characterized by the most unnatural florid style. So, e. g., when Karl Moor realizes his brother's colossal knavery, he regales us with an allegro furioso on the theme Spitzbube, with several variations.[2] Fiesco contributes this inimitable bit when he discovers his murdered wife: "Ah, (mit frechem Zähneblecken gen Himmel) hätt ich nur seinen Weltbau zwischen diesen Zähnen—ich fühlte mich aufgelegt, die ganze Natur in ein grinsendes Scheusal zu zerkratzen, bis sie aussieht wie mein Schmerz."[3] Such examples might be multiplied ad libitum but would serve no purpose. The later dramas furnish more examples of thought soliloquies with the exception of "Die Braut von Messina" in which three of the four soliloquies are of the emotional type. The diction of these soliloquies like that of the entire play is lofty and highly poetic.

Pantomime by an actor left alone on the stage as a means of expressing his emotions has largely supplanted the soliloquy in

1 Jungfrau, III, 6.
2 Die Räuber, IV, 3.
3 Fiesco, V, 13.

the modern realistic drama. Schiller realizes the value of pantomime and frequently inserts stage-directions in his soliloquies calling for it. Yet he does not attempt to supplant the soliloquy by pantomime, but wisely makes it an effective servant. There is but one noteworthy instance where a character is left alone on the stage without delivering the expected soliloquy. The overpowering grief is here expressed by silent pantomime which is far more effective than a long outburst would be. The stage-directions read: "Wallenstein leaves. The servant lights the way. Seni follows. Gordon remains standing in the darkness, looking after the duke until he has disappeared in the furthest corridor; then he expresses his grief by gestures and leans sorrowfully against a column."[1] One of the most common stage-directions found in the soliloquies is that calling for silence, which shows that Schiller realized that the mind does not work with clock-like precision and that the flow of thought is frequently interrupted. " Nach einem langen Tiefschweigen; Pause; grosse Pause; in Tiefsinn versunken; bleibt tiefsinnig stehen; geht tiefdenkend auf und nieder," are the most frequently used directions and are especially numerous in the first four plays. All of the eight directions found in " Wallenstein " and the succeeding dramas call for silence.

Summing up then we find that the soliloquy after running riot in " Die Räuber," both quantitatively and stylistically, gradually subsides and shows marked moderation along both lines. Although " Fiesco " and " Kabale und Liebe " combined do not give as much space to the soliloquy as " Die Räuber," the style employed is still characterized by ranting and florid outbursts and the tendency towards sane expression is slight indeed. In " Don Karlos " on the other hand, the style of the soliloquies is natural and free from ornamentation. In the later dramas in spite of the fact that they are clothed in verse, the prevalence of natural diction and the comparative absence of rhetorical embellishments in the soliloquies is noteworthy. The most striking fact about the soliloquies however is their dramatic form. Practically only such passages as embody philosophic

[1] Wallensteins Tod, V, 5 end.

generalizations might be termed undramatic, all others throb with life. Schiller is especially happy in his use of the dialog form, in his habit of making the soliloquy a real speaking to one's self. When this duality of the speaker is not in evidence the skillful use of apostrophe again imparts this dialog element to the speeches. Question and answer, exclamations and apostrophe never permit the soliloquy to degenerate into a lifeless narration of facts and feelings.

4. Goethe

Unquestioning acceptance of the soliloquy in all its forms characterizes Goethe's use of the convention. In his second dramatic effort, " Die Mitschuldigen," which shows a profusion of soliloquies and asides, Goethe seems to have seen the absurdity of this prodigality and pokes fun at it by saying: " Ohne viel Raison giebt's manchen Monolog."[1] Although his second version of " Götz " contains fewer soliloquies than the first, it is not due to the fact that the soliloquies troubled him, but rather to the fact that Adelheid had been too much in the limelight and had become too prominent in the play. In order to readjust the play and lessen the emphasis placed upon this character, some of the soliloquies were discarded. On the other hand, the first part of " Faust " is richer in soliloquies than the original version known as the " Urfaust." The gradual elimination of soliloquies noticeable in Schiller is not in evidence in Goethe's dramas; quite the contrary, Goethe's later plays employ this convention more freely if anything than the early dramatic works. The most notable change in the soliloquies as we follow the plays chronologically is the gradual transition from a dramatic mold to one that is lyric and elegiac.

Initial exposition soliloquies are employed in " Die Geschwister," " Iphigenie," and " Faust." Of the three only that in the first mentioned is baldly expositional, and it is rather crudely epic, being relieved only by an expression of the speaker's love for Marianne in the form of an impassioned apostrophe and the portrayal of the doubts that arise in his mind as to her love for

[1] III, 8.

him. The conflicting emotions and his decision are dramatically depicted: "O Marianne! wenn du wüsstest, dass der, den du für deinen Bruder hältst, dass der mit ganz anderm Herzen, ganz andern Hoffnungen für dich arbeitet! . . . Vielleicht! . . . Ach! Es ist doch bitter . . . Sie liebt mich . . . ja, als Bruder . . . Nein, pfui! das ist wieder Unglaube, und der hat nie was Gutes gestiftet. . . . Marianne! ich werde glücklich sein, du wirst's sein, Marianne!" The initial soliloquy in "Iphigenie" on the other hand is so permeated with her grief, her unhappiness and her hopes, not to forget the philosophical admixture, that the expositional matter is hidden by a veil, as it were. The exposition in Faust's soliloquy is also entirely subordinated to the emotional element. After revealing his hopeless mood, his dissatisfaction with his present condition: "Es möchte kein Hund so länger leben," the soliloquy reveals his ardent longing for life and love. Realizing his failure as a scholar, Faust casts aside that hitherto dominant interest and pleads for emotional participation in life. The grim bitterness of the introduction gives way to a passage of great lyric warmth and beauty which is followed by another outburst of disgust and the execution of the plan to call magic to his aid. The approach of the Erdgeist is very vividly described, especially where he arouses himself with almost superhuman effort: "Du musst! du musst, und kostet es mein Leben!" The speech then is rather an exposition of mental state than of facts, a highly subjective soliloquy. Epimetheus's opening soliloquy in "Pandora" might also be termed a soliloquy of mental state, as it is for the most part reflective and only incidentally expositional. The bit of self-identification in this speech is interesting:

"Denn Epimetheus nannten mich die Zeugenden,
  Vergangnem nachzusinnen, Raschgeschehenes
  Zurückzuführen, mühsamen Gedankenspiels,
  Zum trüben Reich gestalten-mischender Möglichkeit."

In a few of the fragments expositional soliloquies are found, e. g., in "Nausikaa," I, 2, where Ulysses briefly alludes to his wanderings; in "Die Aufgeregten" and in "Bruchstücke einer Tragödie" which was not written out but merely outlined.

The third act of the second part of "Faust" opens with an expositional soliloquy by Helena in the style of a Greek tragedy.

Instances of identification are rare in the soliloquies. Aside from the example in "Pandora," in which Epimetheus introduces himself, there are two instances in the second part of "Faust," in which Erichtho and Helen introduce themselves. In the opening soliloquy of "Iphigenie" and the first soliloquy in "Nausikaa" the identity of the speaker is revealed without the actual mentioning of the name.

The best of the few examples of self-characterization is that of Brackenburg in "Egmont," in which he contrasts his boyish traits with his present characteristics.[1] But even this forms but a small part of a reflective soliloquy, as is the case with the other characterizing bits, e. g., "Ich habe nicht gelernt zu hinterhalten, noch jemand etwas abzulisten."[2]

Descriptive soliloquies are of frequent occurrence, especially in the second part of "Faust," the second act of which has as many as nine of this type. Weislingen's speech as he is dying is only partially relieved by a dramatic expression of remorse at having condemned Götz to death: "Ich bin so krank, so schwach. Alle meine Gebeine sind hohl. Ein elendes Fieber hat das Mark ausgefressen. Keine Ruh' und Rast, weder Tag noch Nacht. Im halben Schlummer giftige Träume. . . . Matt! Matt! Wie sind meine Nägel so blau!—Ein kalter, kalter, verzehrender Schweiss lähmt mir jedes Glied. Es dreht mir alles vorm Gesicht. Könnt' ich schlafen!"[3] Shorter descriptions, especially of occurrences off the stage, are less crude, as, e. g., Lerse's: "Götzen zu Hülf! Er ist fast umringt. Braver Selbitz, du hast schon Luft gemacht,"[4] or Götz at the window: "Aha! ein rotröckiger Schurke, der uns die Frage vorlegen wird, ob wir Hundsfötter sein wollen."[5] Or "Gott sei Dank! Dort seh ich Feuer, sind Zigeuner. Meine Wunden verbluten, die Feinde hinterher. Heiliger Gott, du endigst grässlich mit mir!"[6] In "Stella" the description at the window is infused

[1] I, end.
[2] Iphigenie, IV, 1.
[3] Götz, IV, 10.
[4] Götz, III, 11.
[5] Götz, III, 16.
[6] Götz, V, 6.

with some dramatic life by an emotional admixture and frequent apostrophes. " So seh ich dich wieder? Den Schauplatz all meiner Glückseligkeit! Wie still das ganze Haus ist! Kein Fenster offen! Die Galerie wie öde, auf der wir so oft zusammen sassen! Merk dir's Fernando, das klösterliche Ansehn ihrer Wohnung, wie schmeichelt es deinen Hoffnungen."[1] In " Egmont " the princess rather baldly describes the unsettled condition of the Netherlands,[2] but later in the same play Alba delivers a dramatic description at the window: " Er ist es! Egmont!—Trug dich dein Pferd so leicht herein und scheute vor dem Blutgeruche nicht, und vor dem Geiste mit dem blanken Schwert, der an der Pforte dich empfängt?—Steig ab!— So bist du mit einem Fuss im Grab! und so mit beiden!—Ja, streichl' es nur und klopfe für seinen mutigen Dienst zum letzten Male den Nacken ihm—Und mir bleibt keine Wahl."[3] Eugenie's description of the preparations made for her departure,[4] Faust's descriptive bits in his first two soliloquies, his rapturous outburst after seeing Gretchen, Gretchen's description of the jewels, all are enlivened by an emotional admixture. The descriptive soliloquies in the second part of " Faust " on the other hand are quite undramatic and unnecessarily retard the action. A few of these speeches are characterized by great stylistic beauty and their marvellous word painting makes one forget their dramatic shortcomings. For example:

" In Dämmerschein liegt schon die Welt erschlossen
Der Wald ertönt von tausendstimmigem Leben,
Tal aus, Tal ein ist Nebelstreif ergossen,
Doch senkt sich Himmelsklarheit in die Tiefen,
Und Zweig' und Äste, frisch erquickt, entsprossen
Dem duft'gen Abgrund, wo versenkt sie schliefen;
Auch Farb' an Farbe klärt sich los vom Grunde,
Wo Blum' und Blatt von Zitterperle triefen,
Ein Paradies wird um mich her die Runde."[5]

1 Stella, I, 2.
2 Egmont, I, 2.
3 Egmont, IV, 2.
4 Die Natürliche Tochter, V, 6.
5 Faust, Part II, 1, opening sol.

6

Faust's opening soliloquy in the fourth act is another instance of lyric beauty. Other speeches however lack the saving grace of formal beauty, as, e. g., Mephisto's soliloquy in the second act:

> "Blick' ich hinauf, hierher, hinüber,
> Allunverändert ist es, unversehrt;
> Die bunten Scheiben sind, so dünkt mich, trüber,
> Die Spinneweben haben sich vermehrt;
> Die Tinte starrt, vergilbt ist das Papier;
> Doch alles ist am Platz geblieben;
> Sogar die Feder liegt noch hier,
> Mit welcher Faust dem Teufel sich verschrieben.
> Ja! tiefer in dem Rohre stockt
> Ein Tröpflein Blut, wie ich's ihm abgelockt."[1]

Purely narrative soliloquies are infrequent, and it is exceptional to find such an ad spectatores speech as Sickingen's: "Es geht alles nach Wunsch; sie war etwas bestürzt über meinen Antrag und sah mich vom Kopf bis auf die Füsse an; ich wette sie verglich mich mit ihrem Weissfisch. Gott sei Dank, dass ich mich stellen darf. Sie antwortete wenig und durcheinander; desto besser!"[2] Epimetheus's second soliloquy in "Pandora," in which he relates his first meeting with Pandora at some length is entirely narrative. But generally the narrative passages are brief and form but a portion of some other type of soliloquy, as in "Iphigenie," where this narrative bit is incorporated in a reflective soliloquy:

> "Jetzt gehn sie, ihren Anschlag auszuführen,
> Der See zu, wo das Schiff mit den Gefährten
> In einer Bucht versteckt aufs Zeichen lauert,
> Und haben kluges Wort mir in den Mund
> Gegeben, mich gelehrt, was ich dem König
> Antworte, wenn er sendet und das Opfer
> Mir dringender gebietet."[3]

Marthe's recital of her husband's desertion,[4] Brackenburg's mention of his attempted suicide,[5] Sophie's mention of her

---

[1] Faust, Part II, II, beg.
[2] Götz, III, 4.
[3] IV, 1.
[4] Faust, I, p. 128, ed. by Heinemann.
[5] Egmont, I, end.

marriage with Söller,[1] Breme's narration of his plans,[2] are other instances of the above mentioned amalgamation of a narrative passage with a reflective or some other type of soliloquy.

Soliloquies whose prime purpose is to acquaint us with the speaker's intention are infrequent. For the most part the intention is the result of reflection or inner conflict and is made a mere appendix to a soliloquy of that type, as was the custom in Lessing and Schiller. Egle's soliloquy in "Die Laune des Verliebten" illustrates the purely intentional type:

"Schon gut! Wir wollen sehn! Schon lange wünscht' ich mir
Gelegenheit und Glück, den Schäfer zu bekehren.
Heut wird mein Wunsch erfüllt; wart' nur, ich will dich lehren
Dir zeigen, wer du bist; und wenn du dann sie plagst!"[3]

Or Götz's: "Wir wollen ihre Geduld fürn Narren halten, und ihre Tapferkeit sollen sie mir an ihren eigenen Nägeln verkauen."[4] Practically every drama has examples of soliloquies with intentional appendices, generally soliloquies of the reflective type.[5] In "Götz," e. g., Franz after comparing Maria and Adelheid in a reflective soliloquy ends with: "Mein Herr muss hin! Ich muss hin! Und da will ich mich wieder gescheit oder völlig rasend gaffen."[6] Or Mephistopheles, after reflecting about reason and science and Faust's character, announces his intention as follows:

"Den schlepp' ich durch das wilde Leben,
Durch flache Unbedeutenheit,
Er soll mir zappeln, starren, kleben,
Und seiner Unersättlichkeit
Soll Speis' und Trank vor gier'gen Lippen schweben;"[7]

1 Die Mitschuldigen, I, 3.
2 Die Aufgeregten, I, 5.
3 Die Laune des Verliebten, Sc. 8.
4 Götz, III, 17.
5 Die Laune des Verliebten, Sc. 5. Die Mitschuldigen, I, 7; II, 5. Götz, I, 2; I, 5; I, end; II, 7; IV, 4. Clavigo, IV, beginning. Die Geschwister, Fabrice's sol., p. 344, ed. Bibliographisches Inst. Egmont, III, beg. Iphigenie, I, 2; II, end. Tasso, III, 5; IV, 3. Natürliche Tochter, II, 2; V, 8. Faust, I, second sol. in scene: Nacht: Studierzimmer (2). Faust, II, V, end of scene: Mitternacht.
6 Götz, I, end.
7 Faust, I, Studierzimmer (2).

The remaining examples of soliloquies containing the speaker's intention are mostly conflict soliloquies in which a decision is reached and the plan of action announced.[1]

Practically all of the reflective soliloquies just mentioned are infused with dramatic life by the judicious employment of exclamations, apostrophes, and the dialog form. This is true even of the later poetic dramas, where the atmosphere of lyric beauty afforded more than a passing temptation to cast the speaker's reflections in a lyric rather than a dramatic mold. With the exception of a few isolated passages, so notably in "Faust,"[2] Goethe successfully combats this temptation and infuses the soliloquies with dramatic vigor. The opening soliloquy in the fourth act of "Tasso" is a splendid example of the dramatic reflective type:

> "Bist du aus einem Traum erwacht, und hat
> Der schöne Trug auf einmal dich verlassen?
> Hat dich an einem Tag der höchsten Lust
> Ein Schlaf gebändigt, hält und ängstet nun
> Mit schweren Fesseln deine Seele? Ja,
> Du wachst und träumst. Wo sind die Stunden hin,
> Die um dein Haupt mit Blumenkränzen spielten?
> Die Tage, wo dein Geist mit freier Sehnsucht
> Des Himmels ausgespanntes Blau durchdrang?
> Und dennoch lebst du noch, und fühlst dich an,
> Du fühlst dich an, und weisst nicht, ob du lebst."

Many of the purely reflective soliloquies are short, as, e. g., Margarete's:

> "Du lieber Gott! was so ein Mann
> Nicht alles, alles denken kann!
> Beschämt nur steh' ich vor ihm da
> Und sag' zu allen Sachen ja.
> Bin doch ein arm unwissend Kind,
> Begreife nicht, was er an mir find't."[3]

Sententious bits are not very numerous except possibly in "Die Mitschuldigen," where there is a liberal sprinkling of

---

[1] Tasso, III, 3. Grosscophta, IV, 1; IV, 8.
[2] Faust, I, V, 602–5; 634–639; 640–651; 672–675; 682–685.
[3] Faust, I, 3211–3216; others 1526–29; 2678–83; 2862–64; 3677–86.

homely practical truths: "Ein Mädchen ist wahrhaftig übel dran! etc.":[1]

"Es braucht's nicht eben just, dass einer tapfer ist;
Man kommt auch durch die Welt mit Schleichen und mit List."[2];
"Es ist ein närrisch Ding um ein empfindlich Blut;
Es pocht, wenn man auch nur halbweg was Böses tut."[3]
"Ja, folgt der Liebe nur! Mit freundlichen Geberden
Lockt sie euch anfangs nach—
Doch wenn ihr einmal den Weg verliert,
Dann führt kein Irrlicht euch so schlimm, als sie euch führt."[4]
"Wenn man was Böses tut, erschrickt man vor dem Bösen."[5]

Weislingen's: "So gewiss ist der allein glücklich und gross, der weder zu herrschen noch zu gehorchen braucht, um etwas zu sein;"[6] Lerse's: "So geht's in der Welt, weiss kein Mensch, was aus den Dingen werden kann,[7] etc.;" Margarete von Parma's: "O was sind wir Grossen auf der Woge der Menschheit? Wir glauben sie zu beherrschen, und sie treibt uns auf und nieder, hin und her,"[8] are on a somewhat higher plane and show a maturer mind.

Philosophical passages in the soliloquies are infrequent. Faust's second soliloquy includes the following philosophical passage:

"Ach! unsre Taten selbst, so gut als unsre Leiden,
Sie hemmen unsres Lebens Gang.
Dem Herrlichsten, was auch der Geist empfangen,
Drängt immer fremd und fremder Stoff sich an;
Wenn wir zum Guten dieser Welt gelangen,
Dann heisst das Bess're Trug und Wahn.
Die uns das Leben gaben, herrliche Gefühle,
Erstarren in dem irdischen Gewühle.
Wenn Phantasie sich sonst mit kühnem Flug
Und hoffnungsvoll zum Ewigen erweitert,
So ist ein kleiner Raum ihr nun genug,

[1] I, 3, v. 181.
[2] II, 1, v. 337.
[3] II, 2, v. 377.
[4] II, 3, v. 398 ff.
[5] III, 1, v. 540.
[6] Götz, I, 5.
[7] Götz, III, 19.
[8] Egmont, I, 2.

Wenn Glück auf Glück im Zeitenstrudel scheitert.
Die Sorge nistet gleich im tiefen Herzen,
Dort wirket sie geheime Schmerzen,
Unruhig wiegt sie sich und störet Lust und Ruh!;
Sie deckt sich stets mit neuen Masken zu,
Sie mag als Haus und Hof, als Weib und Kind erscheinen,
Als Feuer, Wasser, Dolch und Gift;
Du bebst vor allem, was nicht trifft,
Und was du nie verlierst, das musst du stets beweinen?"[1]

Another splendid example is found in Faust's opening soliloquy in the second part, v. 4704–4714.

Soliloquies of violent inner conflict are far more numerous
than the calmer and purely mental deliberative soliloquy which,
as a matter of fact, is very scarce indeed. Weislingen's deliberation after agreeing to remain at Bamberg incidentally depicts the working of his conscience: "Du bleibst! Sei auf deiner
Hut, die Versuchung ist gross—Doch ist's nicht recht, die vielen
Geschäfte, die ich dem Bischof unvollendet liegen liess, nicht
wenigstens so zu ordnen, dass ein Nachfolger da anfangen
kann, wo ich's gelassen habe. Das kann ich doch alles thun,
unbeschadet Berlichingen und unserer Verbindung. Denn
halten sollen sie mich hier nicht.—Wäre doch besser gewesen,
wenn ich nicht gekommen wäre. Aber ich will fort—morgen
oder übermorgen."[2]

In "Die Mitschuldigen," Söller, who needs money to pay his
gambling debts, solves the predicament as follows:

"Ich weiss nicht aus noch ein.
Wie wär's? . . . Alcest hat Geld . . . und diese Dietrich' schliessen.
Er hat auch grosse Lust, bei mir was zu geniessen!
Er schleicht um meine Frau, das ist mir lang' verhasst:
Eh nun! da lad' ich mich einmal bei ihm zu Gast.
Allein, käm' es heraus, da gäb's dir schlimme Sachen—
Ich bin nun in der Not, was kann ich anders machen?
Der Spieler will sein Geld, sonst prügelt er mich aus.
Courage, Söller! Fort! es schläft das ganze Haus."[3]

1 Faust, I, 632–651.
2 Götz, II, 7.
3 I, 7.

Eugenie, on the point of embarking, stops to weigh the pros and cons and decides to remain:

> "Und solche Sorge nähm' ich mit hinüber?
> Entzöge mich gemeinsamer Gefahr?
> Entflöhe der Gelegenheit, mich kühn
> Der hohen Ahnen würdig zu beweisen,
> Und jeden, der mich ungerecht verletzt,
> In böser Stunde hülfreich zu beschämen?
> Nun bist du, Boden meines Vaterlands,
> Mir erst ein Heiligtum, nun fühl ich erst
> Den dringenden Beruf, mich anzuklammern."[1]

"Die Mitschuldigen" contains two splendid examples[2] of the dramatic conflict soliloquy. Although everything points to Sophie's guilt, Alcest is loth to believe that such a noble creature is capable of the theft and is racked by doubt. The opening line of the first soliloquy stamps it as an expression of inner dissension:

> "Solch einen schweren Streit empfand dies Herz noch nie."

In the second soliloquy he is still in the throes of conflict:

> "Nun wären wir gescheit! Das ist ein tolles Wesen!
> Der Teufel mag das Ding nun auseinander lesen! . . .
> Hier ist ein Fall, wo man beim Denken nichts gewinnt;
> Man wird nur tiefer dumm, je tiefer dass man sinnt."

Fernando's terrific mental struggles are admirably portrayed in "Stella," V. 2: "Lass mich! Lass mich! Sieh! da fasst's mich wieder mit all der schrecklichen Verworrenheit!—So kalt, so grass liegt alles vor mir . . . als wär' die Welt nichts . . . ich hätte drin nichts verschuldet . . . Und sie!—Ha! bin ich nicht elender als ihr? Was habt ihr an mich zu fordern? . . . Was ist nun des Sinnens Ende?—Hier! und hier! Von einem Ende zum andern! durchgedacht! und wieder durchgedacht! und immer quälender! immer schrecklicher! . . . Wo's zuletzt widerstösst! Nirgends vor, nicht hinter sich! Nirgends Rat

---

1 Natürliche Tochter, V, 8.
2 III, 7; III, 9.

und Hülfe! . . . Und diese zwei? Diese drei besten weiblichen Geschöpfe der Erde elend durch mich!"

Iphigenie's two conflict soliloquies, IV, 3, and IV, 5, are characterized by a dignified repression which is quite in accord with her nature and fully as forceful as the wild outbursts of an unbalanced nature would be. In the first of the above mentioned speeches she is agitated by the emotions aroused by the base deceit which Pylades urged her to use against her benefactor. After Pylades had persuaded her to adopt his plan Arkas reminded her of the many kindnesses which the king had shown her, and unsettled her:

> " Nun hat die Stimme
> Des treuen Manns mich wieder aufgeweckt,
> Dass ich auch Menschen hier verlasse, mich
> Erinnert. Doppelt wird mir der Betrug
> Verhasst. O bleibe ruhig, meine Seele!
> Beginnst du nun zu schwanken und zu zweifeln? "

In the second speech her wish to leave guiltlessly, so that she may purify her home, struggles against the desire to save her brother and his friend, a course of procedure which involves sacrilege and gross ingratitude. In " Tasso " Leonore passes through a struggle between her selfish and her altruistic Ego, the former demanding that she abduct Tasso, thus depriving the princess of his presence, the latter insisting that she is richly blessed with the good things of this world. After an uninterrupted series of nine questions uttered by her better self her selfish nature presents its arguments in defense of the abduction and is victorious.

> " Ach, sie verliert—und denkst du zu gewinnen?
> Ist's denn so nötig, dass er sich entfernt?
> Machst du es nötig, um allein für dich
> Das Herz und die Talente zu besitzen,
> Die du bisher mit einer andern teilst,
> Und ungleich teilst? Ist's redlich, so zu handeln?
> Bist du nicht reich genug? Was fehlt dir noch?"[1]

The soliloquy is an excellent specimen of a talking to one's self, of a dialog between two well defined characters within one soul.

[1] Tasso, III, 3.

In discussing the emotional soliloquies only the more noteworthy examples will be mentioned, as space forbids a detailed
analysis of this numerous type. Love's awakening and relent-
less rule are most beautifully depicted in "Faust." Faust's
soliloquy beginning:

"Willkommen süsser Dämmerschein!
Der du dies Heiligtum durchwebst.
Ergreif' mein Herz, du süsse Liebespein!
Die du vom Tau der Hoffnung schmachtend lebst, etc." [1]

poetically describes his awakening passion; Gretchen's exqui-
site lyric:

"Meine Ruh' ist hin,
Mein Herz ist schwer;
Ich finde sie nimmer
Und nimmermehr" [2]

pictures Gretchen in the grip of an overwhelming passion.
Subdued grief prevades Iphigenie's opening soliloquy, passionate grief Clavigo's final outburst[3] and Stella's impassioned utterance, V, 1. A mixture of impassioned grief and fear characterizes Gretchen's pitiful appeal in the "Zwinger" scene:

"Wer fühlet,
Wie wühlet
Der Schmerz mir im Gebein?
Was mein armes Herz hier banget,
Was es zittert, was verlanget,
Weisst nur du, nur du allein!" [4]

Jealousy is of infrequent occurrence and is rather gentle than
violent, so, e. g., Brackenburg's speeches, I, end, and V, 3,[5] and
Wilhelm's outburst in "Die Geschwister." Three powerful
instances of fear are Weislingen's deathbed speech,[6] Egmont's
horror of approaching death,[7] and Gretchen's terror-filled wails
in the cathedral.[8]

---

[1] Faust, Pt. I, 2687–2728.
[2] Faust, I, 3374–3412.
[3] Clavigo, V.
[4] Faust, I, 3581–3620.
[5] Egmont.
[6] Götz, V, 10.
[7] Egmont, V, 2.
[8] Faust, I, Dom.

Exuberant joy is the predominating emotion in Tasso's delirious outburst, II, 2, in Stella's soliloquy, IV, 1, and in Eugenie's speech, II, 4.[1] Deep despair hovers over several of Tasso's soliloquies, notably IV, 1, and IV, 5, as well as Klärchen's[2] and Brackenburg's[3] hopeless laments in " Egmont."

Thoas's angry outburst, V, 2, Iphigenie's anxious speech, IV, 1, Fernando's remorseful soliloquy, III, end,[4] Stella's flash of hatred, V, 1,[5] aptly illustrate a few more of the commoner passions.

In classifying the above mentioned emotional soliloquies the predominating passion has been the deciding factor. There are comparatively few soliloquies in which but one emotion is portrayed; quite the contrary is true. The speaker usually veers from one emotion to another or from thought to emotion and vice versa. So in Faust's opening soliloquy we find hopelessness, dissatisfaction, longing, hatred, disgust, despair together with reflective passages. To be sure we do find soliloquies in the crude drama of the early periods which are purely expositional or purely emotional and do not show a combination of thought and feeling. But such instances in classical drama are rare indeed. The division into thought soliloquies and emotional soliloquies, accordingly, has been made solely for the purpose of discussion. In every instance the classification has been made with reference to the predominating element. As Dr. Arnold aptly expresses it: " In the soliloquy, as in every human document, there is a natural intermingling of thought and feeling, and therefore the segregation of thought and passion is an arbitrary arrangement for convenience of discussion."[6]

To sum up, the gradual elimination of the soliloquy in the later dramas, as in the case of Schiller, is not a characteristic of Goethe's craftsmanship. Quite the contrary is true and we find a larger number of soliloquies in the later dramas than those of the earlier period. Another marked difference is the

1 Natürliche Tochter.
2 V, 3.
3 V, 3.
4 Stella.
5 *Ibid.*
6 Arnold, The Soliloquies of Shakespeare, p. 162.

style of the soliloquies of the verse dramas of the two poets. As opposed to the natural diction and the comparative absence of rhetorical embellishments in the soliloquies of Schiller's verse dramas, Goethe's later soliloquies delight in rhetorical figures, stylistic beauty and philosophic reflection. This great formal beauty, however, does not exclude dramatic force and life in all instances, as the soliloquies in "Tasso" and some of those in "Faust," which have already been cited, conclusively prove. Roughly speaking, practically all the soliloquies occurring in the dramas prior to "Egmont" are dramatic and natural in diction, with the possible exception of the soliloquies in "Stella," which are somewhat florid, perfervid and hypersentimental. In "Egmont" the hero's two-page soliloquy, V, 2, is an example of the logically developed and stylistically polished soliloquy that casts vraisemblance ruthlessly aside and aims only at producing a beautiful literary passage. Egmont's premonition and fear of death is the underlying thought, but we are not convinced that a man who can give expression to such figurative and highly embellished language is greatly worried. The other soliloquies of the play are not open to this criticism. Of the dramas following "Egmont," "Tasso" has the most dramatic and least embellished soliloquies, "Iphigenie" and "Die natürliche Tochter" more highly ornate specimens, and at the same time less dramatic, and "Faust," especially the second soliloquy of the First Part and most of the soliloquies of the Second Part, the most beautiful and embellished but at the same time least dramatic soliloquies. The successful employment of the dialog form (sich mit sich selbst besprechen), of apostrophes and a judicious infusion of passion into the soliloquies, raises very many of them to the level of dialog. Those of the soliloquies which are undramatic, notably the descriptive soliloquies, are doubtless dramatic slips, but they have the saving grace of being beautiful errors.

CHAPTER IV

THE ROMANTIC DRAMA

1. *Heinrich von Kleist*

Inasmuch as Tieck, Arnim and Brentano produced only closet dramas there is nothing to be gained by subjecting this dramatic output to an examination. Let us turn then to the real dramatists of the period, beginning with Kleist.

Kleist's latest biographer, H. Meyer-Benfy, in discussing his dramatic technic as applied to the soliloquy, writes: " Kleist differs from all earlier forms of the drama by the remarkably sparing use of the soliloquy. Neither Shakespeare nor Schiller has been his model in this respect. He has consistently scorned the convenient and superficial expedient of French drama, viz., conversations with a confidant. It is greatly to his credit that he got along practically without soliloquies in spite of this fact. It is one of the most noteworthy advances which dramatic art owes to Kleist, an advance which for the time being exerted no influence and which the mature Ibsen therefore had to acquire anew."[1]

This must be taken with a grain of salt. The statement concerning the scarcity of soliloquies certainly does not apply to " Käthchen von Heilbronn " which not only discloses a goodly supply of soliloquies, more than Schiller's " Tell," e. g., but also a painful crudeness in the technic of the same. That Kleist got along without a confidant is true, to be sure, but does this place him on a higher plane than his predecessors? Lessing made use of this expedient only in his early unimportant dramatic efforts, which were under French influence, discarding it in his later works. Schiller did not employ it and Goethe only in " Götz," in which Adelheid's maid may be regarded as a confidant. Kleist deserves credit for his avoidance of the confidant, but it is not necessary to make so much ado about it. To what fact

[1] Das Drama Heinrich von Kleists, Vol. 1, p. 96 ff.

is the scarcity of soliloquies to be attributed? To the fact that the characters are people of action rather than people given to thought and reflection. In such characters thought soliloquies are naturally out of place. Would Kleist have written "Tasso" without soliloquies?

In "Der zerbrochene Krug" no soliloquies occur, although there are as many as sixteen asides. The lack of soliloquies is a necessary outgrowth of the action, all of which takes place in a courtroom in which two or more characters are always present, so that the number of people on the stage makes a soliloquy impossible. In "Penthesilea," that undramatic portrayal of passion run riot, there are also no soliloquies, although a few short speeches of Penthesilea might be regarded as such, inasmuch as she pays absolutely no attention to those about her. This is especially true when she is at the height of her frenzy, so e. g. in scenes 19 and 20. Accordingly only four plays, viz., "Die Familie Schroffenstein," "Käthchen von Heilbronn," "Die Hermannsschlacht," "Prinz von Homburg," and the fragment "Robert Guiskard" need be considered.

At the beginning of the second act of "Die Familie Schroffenstein" Agnes delivers a rather puzzling speech. At first sight it seems to be a soliloquy which the speaker delivers for the benefit of Ottokar, who has entered, and has been observed by the speaker. Inasmuch as the stage directions tell us that Ottokar has his back turned when she espies him and that she continues as though she had not noticed his approach, the object of the speech seems to be to create the impression in Ottokar's mind that he is overhearing a bona fide soliloquy. This of course would be an arrant absurdity, as thought can not very well be overheard. As a matter of fact two passages in this speech: "Da ist, zum Beispiel, heimlich jetzt ein Jüngling," and "Ja, dieser Jüngling, wollt' ich sagen, ist heimlich nun herangeschlichen," show that she intends the speech to be a declaration of love, roguishly delivered to Ottokar, who knows that she is aware of his presence because of these allusions to him. R. Franz, who condemns this speech as a most inexcusable type of soliloquy, evidently overlooked these lines.[1]

[1] R. Franz, Der Monolog und Ibsen, p. 54.

Meyer-Benfy states that Kleist scorns the soliloquy throughout this drama and thereby proves himself an independent artist
and born dramatist.[1] Elsewhere, however, he admits that there
are two short soliloquies[2] in the work and proceeds to laud
them to the skies because they are such splendid link soliloquies! It has been pointed out in the discussion of Lessing
that link soliloquies are an expedient of an immature dramatist.
Secondly Meyer-Benfy overlooks a third and rather long soliloquy delivered by Ottokar when he is shut up in the paternal
dungeon,[3] and a fourth soliloquy which Barnabe delivers
while she is chanting her incantations over the witches' kettle.[4]
Ottokar's soliloquy, IV, 3, deserves special mention. He has
interrupted Barnabe in her incantations and suddenly makes a
discovery (a child's finger in the broth) which greatly arouses
him. He is so overcome with emotion that he finds it absolutely
essential to his happiness to unburden himself of a soliloquy,
but unfortunately he can not do it legitimately with Barnabe on
the stage. How does he meet the dilemma? He politely re-
quests her to leave, repeats his invitation twice, and, when she
ignores his three invitations, pushes her out of the room and
proceeds to deliver himself of his soliloquy, now that the conditions are suitable. This surely is a remarkable advance in
the technic of the soliloquy! It remained for Kleist to show
that a fitting place for a soliloquy may be created ad libitum by
the enforced exit of one's partner.

In "Käthchen" we find two soliloquies that display all the
naïve crudity of the old shrovetide plays, soliloquies that almost
lead one to the belief that Kleist had no well-defined ideas on
the subject of the soliloquy and that the good features are
merely accidental. In the first, IV, 2, Count von Strahl takes
the audience into his confidence and narrates a conversation
just held with his servant, then adds a few reflections and ends
with a reversion to his interview with the servant: " Gottschalk,
der mir dies Futteral gebracht, hat mir gesagt, das Käthchen

1 *Op. cit.*, p. 170.
2 P. 97.
3 IV, 5.
4 IV, 3.

wäre wieder da. Kunigunde zog eben, weil ihre Burg nieder-
gebrannt ist, in die Thore der meinigen ein; da kommt er und
spricht: unter dem Hollunderstrauch läge sie wieder da und
schliefe; und bat mich, mit thränenden Augen, ich möchte ihm
doch erlauben, sie in den Stall zu nehmen. Ich sagte, bis der alte
Vater, der Theobald, sich aufgefunden, würd' ich ihr in der
Herberge ein Unterkommen verschaffen; und indessen hab' ich
mich herabgeschlichen, um einen Entwurf mit ihr auszuführen.
. . . ." Later: "Doch rasch, ehe Gottschalk kommt und mich
stört. Dreierlei hat er mir gesagt: einmal, dass sie einen
Schlaf hat wie ein Murmeltier; etc." In the second soliloquy,
V, 2, the emperor very naïvely supplies us with expositional
matter: "Das Mädchen ist, wie ich höre, fünfzehn Jahr alt;
und vor sechzehn Jahren weniger drei Monaten, genau gezählt,
feierte ich, der Pfalzgräfin, meiner Schwester, zu Ehren, das
grosse Turnier in Heilbronn! Es mochte ohngefähr elf Uhr
abends sein, und der Jupiter ging eben mit seinem funkelnden
Licht im Osten auf, als ich, vom Tanz sehr ermüdet, aus dem
Schlosstor trat, um mich in dem Garten, der daran stösst, uner-
kannt, unter dem Volk, das ihn erfüllte, zu erlaben; etc."
In a long soliloquy at the beginning of the second act Count
von Strahl expresses his sorrow at his inability to marry the
plebeian Käthchen, as that would not be "standesgemäss," his
great love for her and his decision to bear up heroically, in
language that is florid, unnatural and unconvincing: "Ich will
meine Muttersprache durchblättern und das ganze reiche Kapi-
tel, das diese Ueberschrift führt: Empfindung, dergestalt plün-
dern, dass kein Reimschmied mehr auf eine neue Art soll sagen
können: ich bin betrübt. Alles, was die Wehmut Rührendes
hat, will ich aufbieten, Lust und in den Tod gehende Betrübniss
sollen sich abwechseln und meine Stimme, wie einen schönen
Tänzer, durch alle Beugungen hindurchführen, die Seele be-
zaubern; und wenn die Bäume nicht in der That bewegt werden und ihren milden Tau, als ob es geregnet hätte, herabträu-
feln lassen, so sind sie von Holz und alles, was uns die Dichter
von ihnen sagen, ein blosses, liebliches Märchen. . . . Käthchen, Käthchen, Käthchen! etc."

The four soliloquies[1] in "Die Hermannsschlacht" are brief and partially enlivened by the use of apostrophe. Two of the four soliloquies[2] in "Prinz von Homburg" are apostrophes, one to Fame, the other to Immortality, and both are cast in florid style. The other two are reflective, that of the prince being tinged with philosophic reflection:

"Das Leben nennt der Derwisch eine Reise,
Und eine kurze. Freilich! Von zwei Spannen
Diesseits der Erde nach zwei Spannen darunter, etc."[3]

Only one of the reflective soliloquies results in a decision, the others having no direct bearing upon the action.[4] The opening speech in the fragment "Robert Guiskard," a chorus by the people, is nothing but a disguised expositional soliloquy, inasmuch as the committee to whom the speech is delivered is thoroughly conversant with all the facts therein set forth.

Not one of Kleist's soliloquies is a real talking to one's self, and the dialog form which is so successfully employed by the classic triad is nowhere in evidence. An occasional use of the apostrophe is all that gives life to the soliloquies. Kleist's sole claim to distinction therefore is his sparing use of the same in three of the four plays. This is counteracted however by the undramatic form of the same and the startling crudity of the soliloquies in "Käthchen" mentioned above.

2. *Franz Grillparzer*

Unquestioning acceptance of the convention as exemplified in the masterpieces of the classic period characterizes Grillparzer's use of the soliloquy. Goethe's influence is visible in the soliloquies of "Sappho," "Des Meeres und der Liebe Wellen," and "Der Traum ein Leben." In "Sappho" the lyric warmth and the formal beauty of "Iphigenie" and "Tasso" are particularly noticeable. Schiller's influence is frequently in evidence, but most clearly so in "Blanka von Kastilien," the whole style and atmosphere of which is Schilleresque. Rather full

[1] IV, 8; V, 7; V, 17; V, 21.
[2] I, end; IV, 3; V, 2; V, 10.
[3] IV, 3.
[4] Homburg, V, 2.

stage directions throughout the soliloquies bespeak his obligation to Schiller, as well as the fact that most of the dramas beginning with " Das goldene Vliess " curtail the powers of the soliloquy, a practice which characterized the later dramas of Schiller.

Initial exposition soliloquies are a favorite device of our poet. Many of the fragments employ this method of attack, so, e. g., " Rosamunde Clifford," " Robert, Herzog von der Normandie," " Drahomira," " Psyche " and " Rosamunde." His two early playlets " Die Schreibfeder," and " Wer ist schuldig ? " both have initial soliloquies, that of the former, however, being very crudely narrative. All the other above-mentioned speeches have the expositional material concealed by the emotional admixture. The same holds true of the dramas which employ this device. In " Des Meeres und der Liebe Wellen " the exuberant happiness of Hero cloaks the expositional matter; in " Blanka " Fedriko's disgust; in " Die Ahnfrau " the count's resignation and gloom; in " Der Traum ein Leben " Mirza's anxiety and unhappiness; in " Libussa " Primislaus's joy. Apostrophes, exclamations, questions and the pervading emotion are cleverly employed in these speeches.

Fedriko's exposition speech[1] throws considerable light upon his character and incidentally reveals his identity in the first line: " Ha Fedriko, dies deine Bestimmung ? " Both of these types are infrequent. Erny's:

" Sie glauben, weil ich selten sprech' und wenig,
Ich könne mich nicht wehren, nicht verteid'gen,
Mein Vater sprach wohl oft: Sie hat's im Nacken!
Ich hab es auch! Ihr sollt noch wahrlich sehn ! "[2]

is a good example of self-characterization, Hero's opening soliloquy another instance of identification.[3]

Narrative passages in the soliloquies are rather infrequent. Jaromir's recital of his murder,[4] Zanga's account of the battle,[5]

---

[1] Blanka von Kastilien, I, 1.
[2] Ein treuer Diener seines Herrn, II.
[3] Des Meeres u. der Liebe Wellen, I, 1.
[4] Die Ahnfrau, V.
[5] Der Traum ein Leben, III, beg.

Gregor's repetition of his conversation with the king,[1] Leon's narrative of incidents on the return trip,[2] Isaak's account of how he escaped the soldiers,[3] are the most noteworthy. Of these the last mentioned is crudely instructive:

> "Ich habe mich versteckt,
> Als sie nach Räuberart das Schoss durchsuchten.
> Am Boden lag ich, in mich selbst gekrümmt,
> Und diese Decke war mir Dach und Schirm."

Hero's and Jaromir's speeches are the only ones that have an emotional admixture and thus escape being purely instructive.

Descriptive soliloquies and passages are much in evidence. Among these there are some passages of wonderful beauty that deserve quotation, especially two by Hero and another by Mirza:

> "Wie ruhig ist die Nacht! Der Hellespont
> Lässt, Kindern gleich, die frommen Wellen spielen.
> Sie flüstern kaum, so still sind sie vergnügt.
> Kein Laut, kein Schimmer rings; nur meine Lampe
> Wirft bleiche Lichter durch die dunkle Luft."[4]

> "Wie schön du brennst, O Lampe, meine Freundin!
> Noch ist's nicht Nacht, und doch geht alles Licht,
> Das ringsumher die laute Welt erleuchtet,
> Von dir aus, dir, du Sonne meiner Nacht."[5]

> "Abend ist's, die Schöpfung feiert,
> Und die Vögel aus den Zweigen,
> Wie beschwingte Silbergklöckchen,
> Läuten ein den Feierabend,
> Schon bereit, ihr süss Gebot,
> Ruhend, selber zu erfüllen.
> Alles folget ihrem Rufe,
> Alle Augen fallen zu;
> Zu den Hürden zieht die Herde,
> Und die Blume senkt in Ruh
> Schlummerschwer das Haupt zur Erde.

[1] Weh dem, der lügt, I, 1.
[2] Weh dem, der lügt, V, 1.
[3] Die Jüdin v. Toledo, V, beginning.
[4] Des Meeres u. der Liebe Wellen, III.
[5] Des Meeres u. der Liebe Wellen, IV, 3.

Ferne her, vom düstern Osten,
Steigt empor die stille Nacht,
Ausgelöscht des Tages Kerzen,
Breitet sie den dunkeln Vorhang
Um die Häupter ihrer Lieben
Und summt säuselnd sie in Schlaf."[1]

Zawisch's description of the queen, followed by a brief survey
of the state of affairs,[2] is decidedly more dramatic, as is Phryx-
us's description of the unruly barbarians,[3] and Jason's picture
of the vault he has entered.[4] Jaromir's description of the in-
terior of the chapel which is not visible to the spectator is interesting.[5] Accounts of what is going on off the stage also occur
in some of the soliloquies. In "Die Ahnfrau," II, beginning,
Jaromir repeats a prayer which Bertha is delivering in an adjoining room; in "Ottokar," II, 1, Zawisch describes the approach of the queen; in "Der Traum ein Leben," II, 1, Zanga
tells how Rustan is escorting the princess; in "Weh dem,
der lügt," III, 2, Leon describes the adjoining bedroom and its
snoring occupant, and later, III, 3, informs us that Atalus is
digging below the bridge on which he stands.

Purely intentional soliloquies are short and few in number.
Usually they form the appendix to a deflective soliloquy, as was
the case in classic drama. Naukleros's: "Noch geb' ich ihn
nicht auf. Die Freunde samml' ich, wir halten ihn, und wär'
es mit Gewalt,"[6] illustrates the purely intentional speech.
Sappho's soliloquy at the beginning of the fourth act is a good
example of a reflective soliloquy with an intentional ending.
After lengthy reflections about ingratitude and her plans with
regard to Phaon she decides to send Melitta away, inasmuch
as the latter had estranged Phaon from her:

"Nach Chios soll Melitta hin, . . . So sei es! Ha, so sei's!"

[1] Der Traum ein Leben, I, 1.
[2] Ottokar's Glück u. Ende, III, beg.
[3] Der Gastfreund.
[4] Die Argonauten, I, 2.
[5] Die Ahnfrau, V.
[6] Des Meeres u. der Liebe Wellen, IV, 2. Other examples; Libussa, I,
1. Die Argonauten, I, 1, end; Der Traum ein Leben, IV, 4, Rustan's
speech.

In "Die Jüdin von Toledo" the king interrupts his own reflections with the words:

> "Allein was soll das Grübeln und Betrachten,
> Gut machen heisst's; damit denn fang' ich an."[1]

Jaromir's: "Ha, er geht, er geht! . . . Was soll ich? Sei es denn! . . . Nun Fassung, Fassung!"[2] is a noteworthy example of conciseness, as the two lines contain, first, exposition, secondly a conflict, thirdly a decision, fourthly an exhortation to himself to gain composure.

Hero's long soliloquy in the third act is a splendid example of a dramatic reflective speech, dramatic in structure as it abounds in apostrophes, exclamations and questions addressed to herself, dramatic in content as it throws considerable light upon her character. The fact that it is a thought soliloquy is emphasized by the words: "Gedanken, bunt und wirr, durchkreuzen meinen Sinn." Bertha's sad reflective soliloquy, "Ahnfrau," III, 1, illustrates the lyric type:

> "Liebe, das sind deine Freuden,
> Das, Besitz, ist deine Lust?
> Wie sind dann der Trennung Leiden,
> Und wie martert der Verlust?"

Medea's review of her past life, "Medea," IV, Milo's remarks about Jason's changed character, "Argonauten," IV, 2. Leon's reflections on the manner in which he has carried out the injunction not to prevaricate, "Weh dem, der lügt," V, are some of the more striking examples of this type.

Sententious and philosophic ingredients are met with in many of the soliloquies, both in the early works and the later dramas. The unhappy lot of woman is the theme of a serio-comic outburst in "Wer ist schuldig?" the gist of which is embodied in:

> "Genug! In Wien, wie in dem Lande der Chinesen,
> Ist eine Frau das unglücksel'gste aller Wesen!"[3]

as well as of Sappho's sad reflections beginning:

---

[1] IV, 4.

[2] I, near end. Other examples with intentional end: Des Meeres u. der Liebe Wellen, IV, 1, priest's soliloquy; Die Argonauten, I, 1, Medea.

[3] I, beginning.

"Nach Frauenglut misst Männerliebe nicht,
Wer Liebe kennt und Leben, Mann und Frau."[1]

Phaon's dictum on the realization of wishes,[2] Medea's on the folly of man,[3] Primislaus's on the relative position of man and woman,[4] the king's on honor and reputation,[5] bishop Gregor's sermon on truth,[6] are some of the more striking illustrations.

Deliberative soliloquies of the type made famous by Nathan and Posa do not occur in Grillparzer's dramas. The nearest approach is the short speech of the escaping Queen in " Ein treuer Diener seines Herrn ":

"Stell' ich den Meutern mich
Als Königin entgegen und als Frau?
Sie spotten mein und tun ihr blut'ges Werk.
Ergreif' ich dieses Schwert, den Mantel hier
Und kämpf' als Mann um meine süsse Beute?
Zu schwach! . . . O Gott! Kein einzelner genügt!
Drum dort hinein!"[7]

But even here we have an admixture of fear which removes the speech from the plane of calm thought. The same holds true for Ferdinand's soliloquy in " Ein Bruderzwist," in which the line: " Mir ringen Zweifel selber in der Brust " points to an inner struggle.[8]

Conflict soliloquies on the other hand are well represented. Fedriko's, Maria's and the king's conflict speeches in " Blanka,"[9] especially the first and last, are cast in highly dramatic mold. Jaromir's soliloquy at the beginning of the fifth act of "Die Ahnfrau" depicts him in terrible inner conflict caused by the knowledge that he has murdered his father. The hopeless attempt to appease his accusing conscience is powerfully presented.

[1] Sappho, III, beginning.
[2] Sappho, II, beginning.
[3] Argonauten, I, 1.
[4] Libussa, III, beginning.
[5] Jüdin v. Toledo, II.
[6] Weh dem, der lügt, I.
[7] IV, 3.
[8] V.
[9] IV, 3; V, 5; V, 7.

The mention of a few representative emotional soliloquies will suffice. Bertha's rapturous expression of joy,[1] Sappho's beautiful lyric portraying her grief,[2] Melitta's speech of grief and longing,[3] Ottokar's outburst of remorse,[4] Hero's two expressions of her love for Leander,[5] Matthias's hopeless resignation,[6] are some of the more striking examples found in the plays.

The language of the soliloquies in " Blanka " is extravagantly florid and rhetorical, in " Die Ahnfrau " it becomes lurid and feverish:

> " Und die Angst mit Vampirrüssel
> Saugt das Blut aus meinen Adern
> Aus dem Kopfe das Gehirn."[7]

In Sappho formal beauty characterizes the style. In the remaining plays the tendency towards beautiful expression predominates, although unadorned style is occasionally met with. Occasional examples of repression at times of great emotional stress are interesting forerunners of modern technic. Their scarcity, however, seems to show that they are accidental rather than the result of careful planning. In " Ottokar," IV, 1, the hero, after hearing the insulting remarks of Zawisch and the queen, remains silent and after he has stared at the ground for some time in silence says laconically: " Ist das mein Schatten? —Nun, zwei Könige. . . ." When Bancban sees his murdered wife Erny, he contents himself with a laconic: " O, Erny! O, mein Kind, mein gutes, frommes Kind! "[8] But this is due not so much to the overwhelming grief that befalls him as to the lack of good red blood in his veins. On the whole, then, one is justified in saying that Grillparzer does not reach

---

1 Die Ahnfrau, I.
2 Sappho, I, end.
3 Sappho, II, 3.
4 Ottokars Glück, V, 5.
5 Des Meeres u. der Liebe Wellen, III, IV, 3.
6 Ein Bruderzwist in Habsburg, V, end.
7 II, beginning.
8 Ein treuer Diener, III, end.

the level set by Schiller and Goethe in the technic of the soliloquy, firstly because of the numerous narrative and descriptive soliloquies, secondly because of the infrequency of the dialog element and thirdly because more thought is bestowed upon the garb of the soliloquies than upon their appropriate content.

CHAPTER V

1. *Friedrich Hebbel*

"Hebbel is rightly considered the originator (Stammvater) of the new drama. The endeavor to mirror life in its entirety in drama, to pursue man's inner life to its most secret impulses, proceeds from him. In his technic he remained a follower of the classic writers in the fullest sense of the word."[1] This last statement applies especially to Hebbel's use of the soliloquy. The striking feature of his plays is the frequency of soliloquies and the still greater prevalence of asides. And the cause? Hebbel's proneness to morbid introspection and self-analysis, which is faithfully reflected in his dramas. For him the drama is an opportunity to analyze the characters, to reveal every fiber of the soul, to dissect every emotion and thought. We find practically all the characters suffering from this morbid surveillance of their inner self. The result is that the dramas make a mental rather than an emotional appeal. "The frequency and explicitness of the soliloquies is due to the introspection and especially the self-criticism of the characters. With characters who are so constantly occupied with themselves and pursue their emotions and actions with skeptical scrutiny, it is natural to give expression to their inner life in soliloquy form. Seldom is a soliloquy in drama so justified by the character of the people as in the tragedies of Hebbel. The monological outpourings necessarily belong to the character portrayal of such reflecting, problematic natures."[2] "The greater part of their torments would remain unknown if we did not know how their thoughts acquit and accuse each other in every moment when they are alone."[3] One can not help but feel that this

---

[1] R. Weszleny, Hebbels Genoveva, Berlin, 1910, p. 145.

[2] C. Pfeffer, Die Psychologie der Charaktere in Hebbels Tragödie, pp. 112, 113.

[3] Hanstein, Ibsen als Idealist, p. 52.

morbid introspection is carried too far, that we are listening to the author and not to the character in the play, and that the action suffers from a needlessly exaggerated characterization. But even though we should yield a point and accept these revelations of thought and feeling, we must protest against the numerous epic ingredients in the soliloquies. There are altogether too many bits of self-characterization, too many anecdotes and personal experiences embodied in these speeches.

Hebbel's theory with regard to the use of the soliloquy is set forth in three entries in his diary. In 1838, two years before the completion of "Judith," he made the following entry: "Wenn der Dichter Charaktere dadurch zu zeichnen sucht, dass er sie selbst sprechen lässt, so muss er sich hüten, sie über ihr eigenes Inneres sprechen zu lassen. Alle ihre Äusserungen müssen sich auf etwas Äusseres beziehen: nur dann spricht sich ihr Inneres farbig und kräftig aus, denn es gestaltet sich nur in den Reflexen der Welt und des Lebens." This splendid theory was unfortunately ignored all too often in the frenzy of composition. In 1843 we find this entry: "Monologe im Drama sind nur dann statthaft, wenn im Individuum der Dualismus hervortritt, so dass die zwei Personen, die sonst immer zugleich auf der Bühne sein sollen, in einer Brust ihr Wesen zu treiben scheinen." If Hebbel had only borne this injunction in mind we should have been spared many undramatic soliloquies. We do find examples of this type in his works, but infrequently. His last entry on this topic is made in 1861: "Monologe; laute Atemzüge der Seele." This is diametrically opposed to his earlier definition and indicates a dramatic retrogression. Of course, no objection can be raised to this dictum as a definition, since soliloquies are thoughts and emotions made audible, but it seems to be, in a measure, a justification of self-revealing soliloquies whether cast in dramatic or undramatic mold. Inasmuch as this utterance was made after the completion of all his plays, Hebbel may have had in mind the many lyric soliloquies of the Golo type.

In "Judith" the reflections of Holofernes strike a specially discordant note. He indulges in them both when alone and in the presence of his retinue, at the same time realizing their incongruity, for he turns to his followers with the words: " Ihr wundert euch über mich, dass ich aus meinem Kopf eine Spindel mache und dem Traum- und Hirnknäuel darin Faden nach Faden abzwirne wie ein Bündel Flachs. Freilich, der Gedanke ist der Dieb am Leben."[1] His long self-characterizing speech in the first act, as well as his reflective and descriptive soliloquy in the fifth act, are also artistic blemishes. Nor must we overlook Mirza's loquaciousness, which regales us with anecdotes in the most approved Sachsian manner.[2]

" Genoveva " is fairly swamped with soliloquies and unnaturally long asides, more than a dozen of each variety being delivered by Golo. Of these Berger says: " Er (Hebbel) hat Golo nur halb als objektive Gestalt gebildet, denn dieser Charakter war auch ein Gefäss, in das er die subjektive Leidenschaft ergoss, die er sich vom Leibe schaffen wollte. Daher die lyrischen Monologe, die zuweilen sogar als breite Aparte den bewegt hinstürmenden Dialog unterbrechen."[3] Weszleny[4] also condemns these soliloquies: " Die haarspalterische Seelenquälerei in die Hebbel mit Golo hineingeraten ist, liess ihn auch häufig, häufiger als in jedem andern seiner Werke, der Versuchung, sein Wesentlichstes allein oder beiseite auszusprechen, erliegen. Das Schlimme an den Monologen ist, dass sie durchweg Selbstpsychologie enthalten. Es ist nicht die Selbstberatung, nicht das Überströmen unzähmbaren Gefühls wie bei Hamlet, sondern die ängstliche Selbstbeschauung eines seelischen Wollüstlings, das besonders in den Scenen mit Genoveva störend eingreift."

Initial exposition soliloquies are scarce. The unimportant playlet " Michel Angelo,"—which is directed against the narrow-mindedness of critics who approve only of the products of artists such as already occupy a niche in the Hall of Fame and consistently condemn products of contemporary artists,—opens with a long soliloquy which is for the most part reflective, showing us Michel's attitude towards art and critics. The exposi-

1 Judith, IV.
2 Judith, III, beg.; IV.
3 A. V. Berger, Meine Hamburgische Dramaturgie.
4 R. Weszleny, Hebbels Genoveva, p. 143.

tional material contained in it is highly attenuated, the long anecdote which he relates with great relish having absolutely no bearing on the play. The opening soliloquy in "Agnes Bernauer" does little but inform us of the apprentice's jealousy. A belated expositional soliloquy is found in the second scene of "Ein Trauerspiel in Sizilien," which is also marred by an interwoven anecdote of no consequence.

Holofernes's self-characterizing speech has already been alluded to. In "Genoveva" Siegfried indulges in a beautifully worded bit of character drawing:

> "Ich glaub' ein Mann zu sein, was es auch gilt,
> Nur wenn's zum Scheiden geht, bin ich es nicht,
> Da geiz' ich nach dem tiefsten Schmerz, wie nie
> Nach Lust, da bohr' ich mich in Leid und Qual
> Hinein, wie Bienen in den Blütenkelch,
> Und dann erst, wenn ich, zwischen meinem Weh
> Und dem des andern stehend, wählen kann,
> In welchen Abgrund ich versinken will,
> Besinne ich mich wieder auf mich selbst,
> Und reisse mich, als wär's vom Leben los."[1]

But beauty of form does not justify such an undramatic method of presentation. Count Bertram's violent denunciation of himself at least has the redeeming feature of being dramatically expressed: "So ist's, Jammermensch, so ist's! Bilde dir nicht ein, dass du dich zu tief herabsetzen kannst! Du bist solch ein Aber der Menschheit, das sie knirschend hinzufügt, wenn sie ihre Cäsaren und Napoleone aufgezählt hat. . . . Was bleibt dir? Nichts als die Hoffnung, dass es vielleicht noch irgendwo ein Loch in der Welt gibt, wo ein Kerl wie du, der nur noch ein Ding ist, hingestopft werden kann wie ein Fetzen in einen Fensterriss."[2] Benjamin's portrayal of his good qualities is also enlivened by the use of the dialog form.[3] Instances of one person characterizing another in soliloquy are fairly numerous.

Purely narrative passages are altogether too frequent and crude. Hebbel is especially fond of weaving anecdotes and

[1] Genoveva, I, 1, end.
[2] Julia, I, 6.
[3] Der Diamant, I, 4.

personal experiences that have absolutely no dramatic justification into the soliloquies. A quotation of one of the numerous examples[1] will serve our purpose. In "Maria Magdalena," I, 3, Klara, after narrating what she sees from the window and indulging in a few reflections, suddenly inserts the following: "Einmal sah ich ein ganz kleines katholisches Mädchen, das seine Kirschen zum Altar trug. Wie gefiel mir das! Es waren die ersten im Jahr, die das Kind bekam, ich sah, wie es brannte, sie zu essen! Dennoch bekämpfte es seine unschuldige Neugierde, es warf sie, um nur der Versuchung ein Ende zu machen, rasch hin, der Messpfaff, der eben den Kelch erhob, schaute finster drein, und das Kind eilte erschreckt von dannen, aber die Maria über dem Altar lächelte so mild, als wünschte sie aus ihrem Rahmen herauszutreten, um dem Kind nachzueilen und es zu küssen! Ich tat's für sie!"

Golo's account of how he climbed to the top of the tower,[2] Genoveva's account of her son's behavior,[3] Benjamin's narrative of the trouble the stolen gem is causing him,[4] Preising's two instructive speeches in the fourth act of "Agnes Bernauer,"[5] Agnes's report of the conversation that is being carried on off the stage,[6] are some of the numerous narrative soliloquies found in the plays.

There is a goodly number of descriptive soliloquies, though they are not as frequent as those of the narrative type. Holofernes's unsavory description, "Judith," V, Golo's description of Genoveva as she lies in his arms unconscious,[7] his account of her confession in the chapel,[8] Maria's description at the window,[9] Leonhard's characterization of Mary's father,[10] Jacob's

---

1 Judith, III; V. both by Mirza. Michel Angelo, beginning. Der Diamant, I, 4. Maria Magdalena, III, 7. Der Rubin, II, 4. Trauerspiel in Sizilien, I, 2.
2 Genoveva, II, 2.
3 Nachspiel zur Genoveva, beg.
4 Der Diamant, II, 2.
5 Agnes Bernauer, IV, 1, IV, 3.
6 Ibid., IV, 9.
7 Genoveva, I, 2.
8 Genoveva, III, end.
9 Maria Magdalena, I, 3.
10 Ibid., I, 4.

description of his wife and the jewel,[1] are some examples of this type. Most of these are enlivened by the use of exclamations, apostrophes and an admixture of emotion.

Intentional soliloquies occur, as well as intentional appendices to reflective and conflict soliloquies. The former type is epic and undramatic, as the following will show:

Golo. "Kein Vaterunser will ich sprechen mehr,
Kein Ave, wie ich sonst doch gerne sprach,
Wenn morgens eine erste Lerche stieg,
Wenn abends eine ferne Glocke klang.
Von jetzt an soll mir zum Legendenbuch
Das Leben Siegfrieds dienen, meines Herrn,
Gedenken will ich all der Tugenden,
Der Tapferkeit, des hohen Edelmuts, etc."[2]

Herod's two conflict soliloquies, I, 4, and III, both ending with a decision, are highly dramatic. Judith's morbidly introspective soliloquy, III, culminates in her decision to kill Holofernes; a reflective and descriptive soliloquy of the latter concludes with a statement informing us of his intentions.[3]

Reflective soliloquies of the retrospective type outnumber the philosophic variety. Occasionally the two types, neither one of which is dramatic, are blended into one speech. "Genoveva" and "Julia" are well supplied with reflective speeches of all three varieties.[4] The following speech by Alberto illustrates the intermingling of the two types: "Hätt' ich's vorher gewusst, ich hätte mich widersetzt! Nun ist's zu spät! Aber der hat seine Tochter nie geliebt! Nur das Bild, das er sich von ihr machte! Freilich wer liebt anders! Es ist nun einmal das Schicksal des Menschen, dass man ihn wegen Eigenschaften verehrt und anbetet, verabscheut und hasst, die er gar nicht

---

[1] Der Diamant, I, 2.

[2] Genoveva, II, 3. Other examples: Judith, III, 2. Diamant, I, 5; V, 4. Gyges, II, end.

[3] Judith, V. Other examples: Genoveva, III, 12; Maria Magdalena, III, 1; III, 7. Herodes u. Mariamne, I, 2; IV, 7; Gyges u. sein Ring, III, by Rhodope.

[4] Genoveva, II, 4; III, 6; III, 16; V, 7. Julia, I, 4; II, 1; III, 3. Others: Judith, I; Herodes, I, 2; IV, 6. Agnes B., I, 12; III, 5. Siegfrieds Tod: II, 4; III, 5; IV, 13; Kriemhilds Rache: I, 3; I, 7; II, 6. (All of these soliloquies in the Nibelungen trilogy are short and retrospective.)

besitzt, die ihm von anderen nur geliehen werden!"[1] Golo's soliloquy after he has murdered Drago illustrates the philosophic type:

"Ein Mord! Was ist ein Mord? Was ist ein Mensch?
Ein Nichts! So ist denn auch ein Mord ein Nichts!
Und wenn ein Mord ein Nichts ist, dien' er mir
Als Sporn für das, was wen'ger als ein Mord,
Und also wen'ger als ein Nichts noch ist!"[2]

It is noteworthy that the six soliloquies in " Siegfrieds Tod," four of them reflective, are only thirty-three verses long and that the total length of the six soliloquies in " Kriemhilds Rache" is likewise only thirty-three verses (four of these are reflective).

The philosophical element usually forms but a small component part of a reflective soliloquy, and a long outburst such as Golo's on remorse, V, 7, is scarce.

Although deliberative soliloquies are very rare, Alexandra's speech, II, 2,[3] furnishes a good example, conflict soliloquies are rather numerous. Golo's inner conflicts are sometimes laid bare in unpardonably long and unnatural asides,[4] again in soliloquy form.[5] The asides, however, splendidly illustrate Hebbel's idea of a justifiable soliloquy, viz., that two characters should appear to be speaking. Maria's two conflict soliloquies II, 6, and III, 8,[6] as well as Herod's two previously mentioned speeches,[7] are splendid examples of dramatic craftsmanship. One quotation may be pardoned:

"Warum tu' ich's denn nicht? Werd' ich's nimmer tun? Werd' ich's von Tag zu Tag aufschieben, wie jetzt von Minute zu Minute, bis—Gewiss! Darum fort! . . . Fort! Und doch bleib ich stehen! Ist's mir nicht, als ob's in meinem Schoss bittend Hände aufhöbe, als ob Augen . . . Was soll das? Bist du zu schwach dazu? So frag' dich, ob du stark genug bist,

---

1 Julia, I, 4.
2 III, 16.
3 Herodes und Mariamne.
4 II, 4; III, 4; III, 10.
5 II, 5; III, 5.
6 Maria Magdalene.
7 Herodes und Mariamne, I, 4; III, end.

deinen Vater mit aufgeschnittener Kehle . . . Nein! Nein!
. . . Vater unser, der du bist im Himmel . . . Geheiliget werde
dein Reich . . . Gott, Gott, mein armer Kopf . . . ich kann
nicht einmal beten . . ."[1]

A few of the more striking emotional soliloquies aside from
those occurring in "Genoveva," which illustrate practically
every phase of love and jealousy, are Rhodope's beautiful outcry of grief in "Gyges," III, 1, IV, 1, Klara's pathetic outcry of
remorse, II, 2, her despairing soliloquy, II, 6, and Judith's morbid introspective speech, III, in which she tabulates all the emotions that have swept over her since the beginning of the siege.

Hebbel makes it plain that some of his soliloquies are to be
regarded as thought soliloquies, while others must be taken as
speech soliloquies. So Leonhard interrupts a conflict soliloquy
with: "Da kommt jemand! Gott sei Dank, nichts ist schmäh-
licher, als sich mit seinen eigenen Gedanken abzanken müssen!
Eine Rebellion im Kopf, wo man Wurm nach Wurm gebiert
und einer den anderen frisst oder in den Schwanz beisst, ist die
Schlimmste von allen!"[2] Alexandra, while delivering a soliloquy, stamps it as a speech soliloquy when she says:

". . . Das nicht! Sprich wie du denkst,
Der Pharisäer lauscht nicht vor der Tür!"[3]

On the whole, then, the faults of Hebbel's soliloquies out-
weigh their virtues, the many crudities striking a discordant
note. His technic of the soliloquy is on a considerably lower
level than that of the immortal triad.

2. Otto Ludwig

Ludwig's name is usually associated with that of Hebbel as a
forerunner of modern realistic drama. From the mass of his
plans, sketches and fragments, a veritable mountain of ruins,
but two dramas stand out as really great productions: "Der
Erbförster" and "Die Makkabäer." The continual conflict
between objectivity, which he admired so greatly in Shake-

[1] Maria M., III, 8. Other examples: Diamant: I, 4; IV, 2; V, 4.
Julia, II, 12. Agnes B., I, 1.
[2] Maria Magdalena, III, 5.
[3] Herodes u. Mariamne, II, 2.

speare and sought to press into service, and his natural subjectivity resulted in indecision and unproductivity.

Several of his utterances in his dramatic studies point to Ibsen's technic, especially when he says: "Die günstigste Handlung ist ein einfacher Stoff, in dem eine nicht zu grosse Anzahl durch Gemütsart, Intentionen usw. scharf kontrastierter Personen vom Anfang bis zum Ende auf einen möglichst engen Raum zusammengedrängt sind."[1] Another interesting dictum defines a good drama as really nothing but a catastrophe and its careful motivation through characters and situations.[2]

His theory regarding the soliloquy is set forth in his studies at frequent intervals. Without exception these expressions show him to be a warm friend and admirer of this convention when it acquaints us with the secret thoughts and emotions of the speaker. In a chapter entitled "Der Monolog" he writes: "Wie sehr man über das Wesen des Dramatischen im Irrtum ist, kann die jetzt geltende Regel zeigen: so wenig als möglich Monologe! Es kann keinen grössern Missverstand geben als diesen: denn in Wahrheit lähmt ein Monolog so wenig, dass eben die Monologe das eigentlich Dramatische sind. Nur freilich Monologe im rechten Sinne."[3] He considers a soliloquy proper only when its object is to represent the ethical and psychological content of an event. But when a little later on he states that Shakespeare's and Lessing's dramas are only a series of soliloquies with intervening motives one can but smile at this reductio ad absurdum.

Ludwig boldly asserts that mere pantomime can not reveal the speaker's thoughts and emotions. Shakespeare's characters think aloud as it were, according to him. He goes on to say that in reality only a part of one's thoughts and emotions are expressed, but that Shakespeare brings all this to utterance. "Blosse Gebärden des Schauspielers tun es nicht (die inneren Zustände zu versinnlichen und dem Zuhörer mitzuteilen), und der Phantasie des Zuschauers kann man nicht zumuten, die Pausen zu ergänzen."[4]

[1] Dramatische Studien, in chapter: Dramatische Stoffe.
[2] Ibid., Entwicklung der Situation.
[3] Ibid., Der Monolog.
[4] Ibid., p. 92, ed. by A. Eloesser.

How thoroughly he realizes that the soliloquy is a convention is made clear when he says: "Wo die Natur im höchsten Grade des Affekts stumm ist oder nur einen Hauch, eine Interjektion hervorbringt, da übersetzt Shakespeare den Hauch, den Seufzer, das Stöhnen in einen plastischen längern Ausruf, der die Gefühle zusammenfasst in einen prägnanten Satz."[1]   And again: "Die Entwicklung eines interessanten Charakters ist nur in Monologen möglich."[2]

Before considering Ludwig's technic of the soliloquy in his masterpieces a glance at his earliest dramatic venture, "Hans Frei," a comedy dealing with medieval Nürnberg conditions, is of interest.   His technic of the soliloquy in this play is exceedingly crude, the comedy fairly teeming with soliloquies and asides in the most approved Sachsian manner.   Compared with this play Ludwig's masterpieces show decided progress both in the character of the soliloquy as well as in the remarkably temperate use of same.

In "Die Makkabäer" the second, third and fifth acts are entirely devoid of soliloquies though not of asides.   Lea's two soliloquies in the fourth act are powerful and dramatic depictions of the emotions that surge through her breast.   The first of Judah's two soliloquies, I, end, is reflective and permeated with disgust; the second IV, 1, is descriptive, emotional and intentional and withal dramatic in form, a real talking to himself:

> "Wie Sicherheit hier mit bequemem Flügel,
> Dies Lager brütet. Kein Verhau! Kein Graben!
> Ist Judah tot? Ist er ein Tor geworden,
> Dass man ihn höhnen darf? Geduld, bis dir
> Die ausgefallnen Schwingen wieder wachsen;
> Dann zahl' die neue Schuld ihm mit der alten.
> Nun nach Jerusalem!"[3]

The empty stage at the beginning of the fifth act of "Der Erbförster," followed by considerable pantomime, is an interesting forerunner of present day realistic methods.   The short

[1] Dramatische Studien, p. 138.
[2] *Ibid.*, p. 139.
[3] IV, 1.

7

soliloquy which follows is a dramatic translation of her anxious thoughts into words. The eight soliloquies are all short and dramatic. Exclamations, questions, often a real talking to one's self, characterize these soliloquies. The expositional element is very infrequent,[1] most of the speeches being reflective or emotional. The announcing of the approaching actor is a favorite device, as it was with Lessing. Stein's soliloquy, II, beginning, illustrates many of the above mentioned characteristics:

"Verwünschter alter Eigensinn! Der ganze schöne Tag verdorben. Jetzt sässen wir bei Tisch. Recht mag er schon haben, dass das Durchforsten nicht taugt. Aber muss er mich desshalb so in Rage bringen? Freilich ich müsste klüger sein als er. Meine Hitze war auch mit schuld.—Mich dauert nur die Försterin —und die Kinder. Ich will auch—(Steht auf, setzt sich wieder). Was denn? Eine Torheit mit der andern gut machen? So unüberlegt im Nachgeben sein, wie ich's im Uebelnehmen war? Alter Sprudelkopf! Aber das soll mir eine Lehre sein.—(Kleine Pause, dann steht er wieder auf, nimmt Hut und Stock und wirft beides wieder hin.) Nein, es geht nicht; es geht durchaus nicht. Was? Das war eine Blamage, nie wieder gut zu machen. Diesmal muss er kommen; ich kann ihm nicht helfen. Aber er hat vielleicht schon . . . ist das nicht Möller?"

Summing up then, Ludwig's soliloquies are short, dramatic and legitimately used, i. e., to convey thoughts and emotions which would otherwise remain unexpressed. His fidelity to the convention stamps him as a conservative adherent to classical tradition not as an innovator. Credit is due him however for the avoidance of the crude makeshift of the expositional soliloquy.

3. Ludwig Anzengruber

" Through his healthy realism Anzengruber paved the way in a striking manner for the naturalistic movement that followed, although he has nothing in common with its perversities."[2] According to R. M. Meyer, Anzengruber was recognized as the foremost dramatist in Germany at the time of his death. " With his dramas realism entered upon the stage. His serious

---

[1] IV, 7, Der Erbförster.
[2] Max. Koch, Geschichte der deutschen Literatur, p. 483.

realistic drama is entitled to a position alongside of the serious classical drama, his 'volkstümliche' comedy deserves a place beside the classical comedy of Grillparzer and Kleist."[1]

Examining four representative plays, viz., "Der Pfarrer von Kirchfeld," "Der Meineidbauer," "Die Kreuzelschreiber" and "Das vierte Gebot," we find that Anzengruber's technic of the soliloquy is essentially that of the classical period and in no manner foreshadows the technic employed by the naturalists who followed him. Although he avoids purely expositional speeches, we do find epic admixtures occasionally, and, what is worse, disproportionately long speeches in the dialog which convey expositional material, as, e. g., in "Der Meineidbauer." The gradual presentation of expositional material in the last mentioned play reminds one of Ibsen's technic, but Anzengruber's method is crude and transparent as compared with that of the Scandinavian.

[1] Die deutsche Literatur des 19. Jahrhunderts, R. M. Meyer, p. 659.

CHAPTER VI

RECENT DEVELOPMENTS

1. *Hauptmann*

The technic of the modern German realistic drama, notably
that of its chief exponent, Gerhart Hauptmann, is indebted to
such an extent to Ibsen's technic, that a brief discussion of
Ibsen's technic and its influence upon German drama will not
be amiss. This influence is set forth in a very illuminating
manner by A. von Berger: "Of the different elements which
are amalgamated in Ibsen's mental physiognomy and impart to
it the modern expression, the scientific point of view and manner of presentation and everything connected with it have exerted the most stimulating and fruitful influence upon German
drama. Ibsen, accordingly, was the source of the entire flood
of realistic psychological milieu dramas which has poured over
Germany since the middle of the eighties and has not subsided
yet. Perhaps Ibsen's significance and service for German
poetry is best expressed by saying that he created a form of art,
a style and a technic which has proven itself capable of appro-
priating life as it unfolds itself when seen by modern observ-
ers and analyzed by modern psychologists. The essence of this
technic consists in the exclusion of all theatrical conventions
from the dramatic form which do not correspond to reality.
Its aim is the impression as though we were witnesses of scenes
from life and conversations which are given as though they
were not being listened to. The characters of the old drama
do not entirely ignore the spectator; they say many things for
the sake of the spectator which real people who are thoroughly
engrossed in their affairs could not possibly say. The characters in Ibsen's plays do not seem to suspect that they are figures in a drama performed for an audience. Everything that
smacks of the theater is to be rejected. Above all, then, the
monolog, but also many other things that resemble the mono-

log: asides, conversations in which the characters tell each other things they already know, merely so that the audience will be informed, characterization which in the last analysis is nothing more than the assurance by some one that he has this or that characteristic. The German realists since the eighties have adopted Ibsen's technic and adapted it to their needs.

Striking fidelity to reality, absolute spontaneity, exact motivation even to the most minute detail, these three things define the essence of the dramatic form that has its origin in Ibsen. This form made possible the formation of the realistic milieu drama, whose chief exponent is Hauptmann."[1]

Ibsen shows a decided preference for the analytical drama, in which the action is practically ended before the curtain rises and the greater part of the play devoted to the unfolding of the expositional material—Archer refers to it as the retrospective method—but he also uses the synthetic form in which the action is developed and takes place in the drama, and a combination of the two methods. "Ghosts," "Rosmersholm," "The Wild Duck," and "John Gabriel Borkmann" are types of the analytical drama; "The Comedy of Love," "The Pretenders," "Brand," "Peer Gynt," "Emperor and Galilean" and "The League of Youth" are types of the synthetic drama, and "A Doll's House," "Hedda Gabler," "Little Eyolf" and "The Lady from the Sea" show a mixture of the two types. Ibsen's analytical drama in which the conditions of the soul, "états d'âmes," rather than outward conditions, "états des choses," are represented, exerted a powerful influence upon Hauptmann.

Ibsen's technic in his early historical and fantastic plays in verse was on a friendly footing with the soliloquy. When he turned to the prose tragedy of every-day life, however, a change of technic is noticeable. Beginning with "The Pillars of Society," the soliloquy is almost entirely dropped. To be sure a few short soliloquies occur in the last mentioned play and in "A Doll's House," but these cases are exceptional. Here and there we find short outbursts by persons left alone on

[1] A. v. Berger, "Über Drama u. Theater," p. 27 ff., Leipzig, 1900.

the stage, as, e. g., when Hedda burns up the manuscript, end of act III; Hilde, end of act II of " The Master Builder "; Mrs. Borkmann at the beginning of " John Gabriel Borkmann "; Werle at the end of Act I, and Hjalmar in Act V of " The Wild Duck." To all intents and purposes, then, the later plays, the plays whose technic influenced the dramatists of other countries, are devoid of soliloquies.

Ibsen, however, was not the only dramatist who influenced Hauptmann's technic. The influence exerted by the joint production of Holz and Schlaf, " Die Familie Selicke," upon Hauptmann was profound. Especially " Vor Sonnenaufgang," which incidentally is dedicated to Holz and Schlaf, is greatly indebted to the above mentioned tour de force. " Die Familie Selicke " unrolls a page from the seamy side of life just as it might be enacted before an invisible spectator. The naturalistic portrayal of conditions as set forth in this play eschews soliloquies, asides and all remarks ordinarily made for the benefit of the spectator. Both the minute and painstaking depiction of conditions as well as the avoidance of the convention of the soliloquy have undoubtedly left their impression upon Hauptmann's work. A gripping psychological drama, " Meister Oelze," written by Schlaf after the dissolution of the literary partnership, deserves mention. The treatment is naturalistic throughout and but two short outbursts under the stress of the greatest emotion occur.

In discussing Hauptmann's technic of the soliloquy, I shall confine myself to the realistic dramas. With the exception of short emotional outbursts by characters who are left alone on the stage, similar to those found in Ibsen's later dramas, nothing remotely resembling a soliloquy occurs. Bearing in mind that the soliloquy is a convention, we can hardly refer to these brief utterances as soliloquies, inasmuch as it is quite common in every-day life to give vent to short ejaculations when overcome with some emotion. " It happens rather frequently that an excited person soliloquizes. But cases in which this is in accordance with reality are not soliloquies in the technical sense, and even the naturalists raise no objection to them. Only such speeches can be regarded as soliloquies which are delivered on the stage with the assumption that that which we hear is only thought and not really spoken."[1]

What takes the place of the soliloquy in Hauptmann? Are the substitutes which he offers for expositional soliloquies, soliloquies of thought and emotion and conflict, satisfactory? In conveying the exposition Hauptmann follows in the footsteps of Ibsen, who shows remarkable skill in that particular. Setting aside the crude expositional soliloquy, many playwrights resort to the convenient French confidant. Not so Ibsen. Nor does he resort to the naïve expedient of having persons on the stage converse about things which are absolutely familiar to themselves merely to acquaint the audience with them. The return of a friend or acquaintance who has not kept up the correspondence and naturally has to be informed of what has occurred during the interim is a favorite device of Ibsen. Lona Hessel and John Tönnesen return after a long absence in "The Pillars of Society," Mrs. Linde in "The Doll's House," Pastor Manders and Oswald in "Ghosts"; Kroll meets Rebekka after a long interval in "Rosmersholm;" in "The Lady of the Sea" Arnholm and the Stranger return; in "Hedda Gabler" Tesman and Hedda return from a trip, while Thea and Eilert appear after years of absence, etc. This device is also employed by Hauptmann in several of his plays. In "Vor Sonnenaufgang" Alfred Loth visits Hoffmann after an interim of ten years; in "Das Friedensfest" Dr. Scholz as well as his son Wilhelm returns after a long absence; in "Einsame Menschen" Anna Mahr enters a household and disrupts it.

What of the speaker's secret thoughts and aspirations, the torturing doubts and racking conflicts that beset his soul? How are they made known to the audience now that the soliloquy is out of the question? By means of pantomime and facial expression! Elaborate stage directions, sometimes a page in length, are inserted by the author ostensibly for the actor's guidance in the interpretation of inner thoughts, emotions and conflicts by means of facial expression and pantomime. But if as a matter of fact some of the demands made upon facial

[1] Hans Sittenberger, Die Wahrheit auf der Bühne, p. 31, Vienna, 1893.

expression are impossible of execution, as I shall shortly demonstrate, then the stage directions, in part at least, are intended for the reader and are epic, not dramatic. Although pardonable in a closet-drama, this method of procedure is entirely out of place in a drama intended for the stage. And even where the stage directions are capable of execution, the spectator sees things more or less through a veil and has to indulge in conjecture as to what the author is really driving at. I venture to suggest that the actual thoughts, the conflicting emotions themselves are of more interest to the spectator than the mere knowledge that the actor is thinking or passing through an inner conflict.

Some of Hauptmann's stage-directions cannot possibly be executed, while others must certainly tax the ingenuity of the actors to the utmost. In "Vor Sonnenaufgang," e. g., Frau Krause on one occasion is asked to be "blaurot vor Wut," on another "puterrot." In "Das Friedensfest" he makes a demand which only an actor with the characteristics of a chameleon can suitably interpret: "Seine Farbe wechselt oft." Hereupon the much abused face is to show plainly how conflicting emotions rack his soul and how his previously made resolution begins to weaken: "Hierauf is deutlich wahrzunehmen wie Strömungen für und wieder in ihm kämpfen,—wie er in seinem Entschluss wankend wird." Not indistinctly mark you, but plainly! Then, when his father appears, he is asked to portray a violent inner struggle by means of pantomime: "Wilhelm scheint einen Seelenkampf physisch durchzuringen." At the end of the first act of "Einsame Menschen," the stage directions tell us that: "In Käthe ist etwas vorgegangen!" What? And how is this mysterious something to be presented to the audience?

Again the stage-directions are filled with characterizing and descriptive bits which suggest the spurned characterizing soliloquy. The action itself ought to bring out these characteristics. The author is making use of the prerogatives of the novel, he employs the epic method, inasmuch as these statements are intended for the reader, not the spectator in the theater. The directions at the beginning of "Die Weber" are the best example of this undramatic method of procedure: "Die meisten der harrenden Webersleute gleichen Menschen, die vor die Schranken des Gerichts gestellt sind, wo sie in peinigender Gespanntheit eine Entscheidung über Tod und Leben zu erwarten haben. Hinwiederum haftet allen etwas Gedrücktes, dem Almosenempfänger Eigentümliches an, der, von Demütigung zu Demütigung schreitend, im Bewusstsein, nur geduldet zu sein, sich so klein als möglich zu machen gewohnt ist. Dazu kommt ein starrer Zug resultatlosen, bohrenden Grübelns in allen Mienen. Die Männer, einander ähnelnd, halb zwerghaft, halb schulmeisterlich, sind in der Mehrzahl flachbrüstige, hüstelnde, ärmliche Menschen mit schmutzigblasser Gesichtsfarbe: Geschöpfe des Webstuhls, deren Kniee infolge vielen Sitzens gekrümmt sind. Ihre Weiber zeigen weniger Typisches auf den ersten Blick; sie sind aufgelöst, gehetzt, abgetrieben, während die Männer eine gewisse klägliche Gravität noch zur Schau tragen und zerlumpt, wo die Männer geflickt sind." In "Vor Sonnenaufgang" we are informed that Mrs. Krause's deportment and clothing betray pride, stupid arrogance and absurd vanity, also that her face is hard, sensual and wicked; that Hoffman's expression is "verschwommen"; that Kahl would like to play both the gentleman as well as the man of wealth, that his features are coarse and his expression mostly "dummpfiffig."

The most striking example of epic treatment is shown in a direction at the beginning of the second act of the same play which reads: "hierauf die feierliche Morgenstille;" Even a past master of stage effects might well be perplexed at this demand. It would also tax his ingenuity to present a sultry day towards the end of May, called for in the introduction to "Die Weber."

2. Sudermann

In contrast to Hauptmann, who devoted the greatest attention to the portrayal of existing conditions, the milieu, Sudermann's chief aim is a stirring exciting action. Opposed to the negative, passive heroes of the former, Sudermann presents us with positive, active protagonists. In contrast to the messenger from the outside world who attempts to relieve conditions

in Hauptmann's dramas, Sudermann has the hero himself
return from distant parts to stir up a conflict between two con-
tending points of view, as in " Die Ehre," " Die Heimat,"
" Glück im Winkel " and others.

What as to his technic of the soliloquy? In " Die Ehre,"
his first dramatic venture, we find three short soliloquies[1] and
numberless asides; six in the first act, eleven in the second,
twelve in the third and six in the fourth, a total of thirty-five.
The soliloquies are of the reflective type with an intentional ending, thus having some dramatic justification as they affect the
action. The chief blemish of the play are the long didactic
speeches of Trast, the mouthpiece of the author, in the style
of the French raisonneur.

In " Sodom's Ende " soliloquies are fairly numerous. The
author aims this satirical thrust at the soliloquy, when he has
Adah say, I, 10, " Ich überlasse Sie dem Monolog, Herr Professor, den Sie sogleich über unsere Verderbtheit halten werden." Whereupon the professor does deliver a soliloquy,
although he avoids the type suggested. The soliloquies are for
the most part reflective,[2] with one very dramatic conflict soliloquy by Willy between his baser and his better self, ending in
a victory for the latter.[3]

In " Die Heimat," his most effective stage play, the soliloquy
does not occur at all and but three asides are found. The same
noids true of " Johannes," in which but one aside occurs.
" Teja " and " Fritzchen " eschew both soliloquies and asides.

When we turn to the idealistic drama, however, we meet
with the customary technic of the soliloquy. In Hauptmann's
" Die versunkene Glocke," Sudermann's " Die drei Reiher-
federn," Fulda's " Der Talisman," all symbolic dramas, the
convention is employed as it was in the dramas of the classical
period. There seems to be a tacit admission, then, on the part
of the modern realistic playwrights that the soliloquy, however
out of place in realistic drama, has a perfectly justifiable place
in idealistic drama.

[1] II, 10; III, 4; IV, 3.
[2] IV, 5; IV, 16; IV, 17; end of the play.
[3] III, 17.

To round out this discussion it will be necessary to consider briefly two new tendencies in modern German drama, one revitalizing the Greek drama, the other the Romantic Drama. Hugo von Hofmannsthal's "Elektra" and "Oedipus" furnish the best examples of the former movement. Of the two, "Elektra" shows the closer resemblance to Sophocles's drama of the same title upon which it is based. Strictly speaking, the presence of the chorus in Sophocles's drama makes a real soliloquy impossible, but as a matter of fact, Elektra is so overcome with grief when she delivers her outbursts of sorrow, that she is entirely oblivious of the presence of the chorus and therefore, to all intents and purposes, delivers genuine soliloquies. Later, in the third Epeisodion, when Orestes gives her an urn supposed to contain her father's ashes, Elektra again gives vent to her feelings as though no one were present. In the classic drama we accordingly have what amounts to three soliloquies. In Hofmannsthal's version we find a long morbidly passionate soliloquy, which corresponds to Elektra's first soliloquy in Sophocles's version. It is dramatic in form, practically all of it being addressed to her dead father. Compared with the original, it shows the following points of difference. The comparative calm and dignity of the original is translated into torrid passion writhing in lust for blood:

> "So wie aus umgeworfnen Krügen wird's
> aus den gebundnen Mördern fliessen, rings
> wie Marmorkrüge werden nackte Leiber
> von allen ihren Helfern sein, von Männern
> und Frauen, und in einem Schwall, in einem
> geschwollnen Bach wird ihres Lebens Leben
> aus ihnen stürzen."

The description of the murder is given in greater detail and the call for revenge in the original gives way to a bloody description of the manner in which she will avenge her father. Several asides and a short soliloquy of regret occur later in the version.

In "Oedipus" there is little similarity in the two versions, as Hofmannsthal in his drama gives us only the Vorgeschichte of the classical play. Numerous soliloquies occur in this drama, some with a great deal of expositional material in a rather undramatic mold, others reflective and emotional, in which exclamations, apostrophes and questions are employed to good effect.

Hardt's "Tantris der Narr" and Stucken's Grail series consisting of "Gawan," "Lanval" and "Lanzelot," will illustrate the other modern movement. The splendor of medieval knighthood and chivalry, enchanted woods and chapels, moonlit valleys and vile sorcerers are revived in these plays. Soliloquies are not numerous in these dramas. In "Lanzelot," e. g., none whatever occur, the author preferring to let his character indulge in pantomime, where the setting is most propitious for a soliloquy, as in III, 5: "After Lanzelot has gone, Elaine falls upon her knees beside the bed, shaken with sobs. Then she rises, wipes away the tears and goes to the alcove on the right, where she hastily dresses. Suddenly she stops to listen and hurries to the door in the background. Carefully she opens the door and looks out." Occasionally long epic narratives are found, as in "Gawan." Expositional material is not often met with in the soliloquies, which are generally cast in very dramatic form, as, e. g., Gawan's sleep soliloquy, III, his conflict soliloquy, IV, 2, Lanval's longing for his fairy wife, IV, 1.

In the initial expositional soliloquy in "Gawan," delivered by Artus, there is a beautiful descriptive passage addressed to the Virgin:

" Schön warst Du Marie, so erschrocken und kindlich hold!
Alabaster Dein Kinn, Deine Locken gesponnenes Gold.
Und Dein Augenpaar zwei Seen mit blauen Tiefen,
Die selbst nie die Perlen gesehen, die drunten schliefen.
Dein Schneeleib war durchbebt von des Wunders Schauer."

In Hardt's "Tantris," there is but one dramatic soliloquy, in his "Gudrun" four occur, three of them reflective, the other an outburst of anger and grief. Apostrophes and exclamations and occasionally the dialog form are very effectively employed in many of the soliloquies.

Conclusion

Has the recent drama gained in artistic effectiveness by its disuse of the soliloquy? Is dramatic technic improved by the elimination of the convention of the soliloquy? The answer to these questions, which were touched upon in the discussion of Hauptmann, will round out this investigation.

"The history of the drama is the long record of the effort of the dramatist to get hold of the essentially dramatic and to cast out everything else."[1] The naturalistic dramas have cast out the soliloquy and the aside because they have felt both to be unnatural. Their attitude is that of Archer, who says: "A drama with soliloquies and asides is like a picture with inscribed labels issuing from the mouths of the figures. The glorious problem of the modern playwright is to make his characters reveal the inmost workings of their souls without saying or doing anything that they would not say or do in the real world."[2] A glorious problem, indeed! But unless we are endowed with a sixth sense that will enable us to become proficient mind-readers, I fear that these inmost workings of the soul will be shrouded in impenetrable darkness. But, the naturalist will retort, a pause, a look of the eye, facial expression, the actor's actions and pantomime, will convey to the audience what is going on in the mind of the character. It is undeniable, "that for the practical purposes of dramatic presentation, the symptoms of passion can be mechanically mimicked with tolerable precision."[3]

The simple or primary emotions, such as grief, joy, terror, "which have immediate and characteristic outward symptoms"[4] can undoubtedly be revealed to the audience. But what of the more complex and habitual emotions which are rather attitudes of mind and have no characteristic outward symptoms, such as love, hatred, jealousy? Neither the character's attitude nor the conflicting emotions that surge through his soul at a crisis,

---

[1] B. Matthews, The Development of the Drama, p. 321.
[2] W. Archer, Playmaking, A Manual of Craftsmanship, London, 1912, p. 305.
[3] W. Archer, Masks or Faces, London, 1888, p. 199.
[4] W. Archer, op. cit., p. 207.

to say nothing of his inner thoughts, can be revealed to the audience by means of facial expression or pantomime. " The conflicting emotions of a hero at the crisis of his fate can not possibly be made known except out of his own mouth."[1] " The soliloquy in which a character speaks boldly of his most secret thoughts lets a tortured hero unpack his heart; it opens a window into his soul and it gives the spectator a pleasure not to be had otherwise."[1] I quite agree with Robert Hessen when he says: " I have witnessed enough pantomimes in my lifetime to know that they are significant only where nothing at all is to be expressed and every laboring man would understand the crude stuff. Where something worth while is to be conveyed the understanding ceases and the libretto is pressed into service. And along this line lies the development of the drama when every soliloquy is dropped. On the stage pantomime; the audience with their noses buried in books, that is known by the name of 'modern dramas.'"[2] Speaking of a performance of " Francillon " he says: " The impersonator of Lucien groped about the stage for minutes in absolute silence and the audience sat there with gaping mouths without having the slightest idea of what it was all about."[2]

If, accordingly, a character's inmost thoughts and his inner conflicts can not be expressed even adequately by means of the substitute which the naturalists have offered, viz., pantomime, then the dramatist is handicapped by the loss of the soliloquy, and dramatic technic is made less effective. If the drama loses in artistic power by the elimination of this convention, it is high time that the dramatists of today protest against its disuse and emphasize the protest by again employing it. " Artistic and art-loving painters and sculptors would scornfully reject such a proposition as the following: 'Yes you may paint, but you must no longer use blue or yellow,' or, 'Yes, indeed, you may make statues of women, but only with a veil, like the fellah women in Egypt. The upper part of the nose and the eyes may be visible, but no more. If you are any sort of artist you will be able to make a very expressive face in spite of this re-

[1] B. Matthews, A Study of the Drama, pp. 148–149.

[2] Dr. Robert Hessen (Avonanius), Dramatische Handwerkslehre, Berlin, 1902, pp. 232–233.

striction.' "[1] The simple fact that naturalists have lost their taste for soliloquies is no reason why every one else should dislike them. Their reiteration of the demand that everything on the stage should be a faithful copy of life is absurd, inasmuch as practically everything connected with a performance on the stage rests upon conventions. Even in a prose play based upon every-day life, there is readjustment of the plot, a compression as it were, so that it will fit into the two or three hours set aside for the performance, the elucidation of the plot so that it becomes clear to the spectator, the condensation and heightening of the dialog. Then there is the removal of the fourth wall, the raising of the actor's voices, the selection and heightening or emphasizing of gesture and facial play. "Everyone knows that the actor is not necessarily a mere copyist of nature; he must always imitate, though we may permit him to steep his imitation, so to speak, in a more or less conventional atmosphere." "He plays naturally," or, in other words, "He imitates well" is our highest formula of praise even for the operatic tenor or the French tragedian, who may not deliver a single word or tone exactly as it would be uttered in real life.[2]

Inasmuch as the convention of the soliloquy, then, is but one of many, the singling out of, and the attack upon, this one convention is uncalled for and illogical. If the characters must not do or say anything that they would not do or say in the real world, then let the gentlemen of the naturalistic school be consistent and eliminate all the other numerous conventions. No defense of the expositional soliloquy is intended or implied in the preceding remarks. It is, as Mr. Archer aptly calls it, a slovenliness, and all critics are agreed that it must be shunned. But when Mr. Archer suggests that "a conversation on the telephone often provides a convenient and up-to-date substitute for a soliloquy,"[3] does he suppose that an up-to-date audience will fail to see through the thin disguise and not regard this makeshift with an amused smile?

It is interesting to note that Mr. Archer, after denouncing the soliloquy as a "slovenliness" and "a disturbing anachro-

---

[1] R. Hessen, *op. cit.*, p. 232.
[2] W. Archer, *Masks or Faces*, p. 196.
[3] W. Archer, *Playmaking*, p. 305.

nism," suffers a change of heart and champions the poor down-trodden outcast by approving of the emotional and conflict soliloquy. His attitude, especially if it reflects the point of view of the naturalists, augurs well for the future of the soliloquy and points to a new lease of life for it. In answer to his question: "Are there in modern drama any admissible soliloquies?"[1] he writes: "A few brief ejaculations of joy or despair, are, of course, natural enough and none will cavil with them. The approach of mental disease is often marked by a tendency to unrestrained loquacity, which goes on while the sufferer is alone, and this distressing symptom may, on rare occasion, be put to artistic use. (Gryphius was the first to advance this idea.) Short of actual derangement, however, there are certain states of nervous excitation which cause even healthy people to talk to themselves, and if an author has the skill to make us realize that his character is passing through such a crisis, he may risk a soliloquy, not only without reproach but with conspicuous psychological justification."[1] The last part of this statement bears out Brander Matthews's remark that "the conflicting emotions of a hero at the crisis of his fate can not be made known except out of his own mouth." The vulnerable part of his dictum lies in the fact that he attempts to convert a convention into a faithful reproduction of life. The thoughts and emotions of a character at a crisis would rarely if ever be expressed in real life other than by gestures and facial expression and possibly by brief ejaculations. If then, the character on the stage indulges in a soliloquy, it is because the author is making thought audible for our benefit by means of the convention of the soliloquy which permits inaudible thought to become audible. At any rate, Mr. Archer has seen the necessity of informing the audience of what goes on in the minds of the characters, and that is a decided step in advance of the naturalists, who have been unsuccessful in conveying such information by means of pantomime.

It is to be hoped that the dramatic authors of today and tomorrow will realize that the elimination of the soliloquy of thought and feeling is a loss to the drama and that their restoration will increase its artistic effectiveness.

[1] W. Archer, Playmaking, p. 306 ff.

BIBLIOGRAPHY

Anzengruber, L., Dramas of.

Archer, W., English Dramatists of Today, London, 1882.
  Masks or Faces, London, 1888.
  Playmaking, London, 1912.

Arnold, L. M., The Soliloquies of Shakespeare, N. Y., 1912.

Ayrer, J., Selected Plays of.

Berger, A. v., Meine Hamburgische Dramaturgie, Wien, 1910.
  Über Drama und Theater, Leipzig, 1900.

Creizenach, W., Die Schauspiele der englischen Komödianten, Berlin, 1889.
  Geschichte des neueren Dramas, Halle, 1893.

Devrient, E., Geschichte der deutschen Schauspielkunst, 1848.

Drama des Mittelalters, 3 vols., ed. by R. Froning Stuttgart, 1891.

Düsel, F., Der dramatische Monolog in der Poetik des 17 und 18. Jahrhunderts und in den Dramen Lessings, Hamburg, 1897.

Franz, R., Der Monolog und Ibsen, Marburg, 1907.

Freytag, G., Technik des Dramas, 10th edition, Leipzig, 1905.

Fulda, L., Der Talisman.

Gartelmann, H., Dramatik, Berlin, 1892.

Gengenbach, P., Die Totenfresser. Die zehn Alter dieser Welt.

Glock, A., Die Bühne des Hans Sachs, Passau, 1903.

Goethe, J. W., Dramas of.

Gottschall, R. v., Zur Kritik des modernen Dramas, Berlin, 1900.

Gottsched, J. C., Versuch einer kritischen Dichtkunst, 1730.
  Cato.

Grillparzer, F., Dramas of.

Gryphius, A., Dramas of.

Hamilton, C., Theory of the Theatre, N. Y., 1910.

Hardt, E., Tantris der Narr. Gudrun.

Hauptmann, G., Dramas of.

Hebbel, F., Dramas of.

Tagebücher.

Hédelin, The Whole Art of the Stage Made English, 1684.

Heinrich Julius, Dramas of.

Henderson, A., The Evolution of Dramatic Technic, North Am. Rev., March, 1909.

Hennequin, A., The Art of Playwriting, 1890.

Hessen, R., Dramatische Handwerkslehre, Berlin, 1902.

Hofmannsthal, H. v., Elektra. Oedipus.

Holz, A., Die Familie Selicke. (Holz und Schlaf.)

Ibsen, H., Dramas of.

Kleist, H., Dramas of.

Klinger, F., Sturm und Drang. Die Zwillinge.

Leisewitz, J., Julius von Tarentum.

Lenz, J., Der Hofmeister. Die Soldaten.

Lessing, G. E., Dramas of.

Hamburgische Dramaturgie.

Beiträge zur Historie und Aufnahme des Theaters.

Lohenstein, C., Cleopatra. Ibrahim Sultan.

Ludwig, O., Dramas of.

Shakespeare Studien.

Dramatische Studien.

Matthews, B., The Development of the Drama, N. Y., 1906.

A Study of the Drama, N. Y., 1910.

Concerning the Soliloquy, Putnam's Monthly, Nov., 1906.

Meyer, H., Das Drama H. v. Kleists, Göttingen, 1911.

Müller, Maler, Golo und Genoveva.

Mundt, T., Dramaturgie, Berlin, 1848.

Paull, H. M., Dramatic Convention with Special Reference to the Soliloquy, Fortnightly Review, May, 1899.

Pfeffer, C., Die Psychologie der Charaktere in Hebbels Tragödie, Leipzig.

Rebhuhn, P., Susanna.

Robertson, J. G., Zur Kritik Jakob Ayrers mit besonderer Rücksicht auf sein Verhältnis zu Hans Sachs und den englischen Komödianten, Leipzig, 1892.

Sachs, Hans, Fastnachtspiele; Comedies and Tragedies, selection of.

Schiller, F., Dramas of.

Schlaf, J., Meister Ölze. Die Familie Selicke.

Schlag, H., Das Drama, Essen, 1909.

Schlegel, J. E., Hermann.

Shrovetide Plays of the fifteenth Century, ed. by Keller, Stuttgart, 1858.

Sittenberger, H., Die Wahrheit auf der Bühne, 1893.

Stachel, P., Seneca und das deutsche Renaissance Drama, Berlin, 1907.

Stucken, E., Gawan. Lanval. Lanzelot.

Stürmer und Dränger, ed. by A. Sauer, Berlin, 1885.

Sudermann, H., Dramas of.

Wagner, H., Die Kindermörderin.

Waldis, B., Der verlorene Sohn.

Weise, C., Die böse Catharine. Der Bäurische Machiavellus. Masaniello.

Weszleny, R., Hebbels Genoveva, Berlin, 1910.

INDEX

The Index contains the titles of works and the names of authors mentioned in the text or footnotes of the foregoing treatise.

VITA

The author, Erwin W. Roessler, was born near Stuttgart, Germany, March 17th, 1880. He attended the elementary and high schools of Chicago, Ill., and took his A.B. degree at the University of Chicago in the summer of 1900. From 1900–1901 he took graduate work in Latin at the University of Chicago; from 1906–1911 he pursued courses in the department of Germanic Languages and Literature of Columbia University. In 1904 he became instructor of modern languages in the New York High School of Commerce; since 1908 he has been chairman of the department.

The author is indebted to Professor Calvin Thomas for valuable suggestions given during the preparation of the dissertation.